Bravo!! Paulette's book will whisk you ~~~ ~~~ ~. She walks you down a path of pure life captivation, fully illuminating the very real human experience. She offers such a down-to-home, delicious, moving and inspiring compilation that equally melted and lifted my heart with each page. Enjoy this piece of art!

Laurel Inman, life coach & founder of the Institute for Integrative Coach Training

I loved this book. In this, her very personal debut memoir, Paulette Bodeman carries the reader on a roller-coaster life altering journey unveiling her own vulnerabilities, her engaging sense of humor and her profound love of life. Through the sharing of this story, its imperfections right alongside its triumphs, Bodeman embodies the most important qualities of a great teacher giving her students the truest gift a guru can give... the ability and the knowledge to tackle and best our own demons.

Karen Keilt, author of The PARROT'S PERCH

Sharing one's story with naked authenticity is perhaps the most sincere gift of love anyone can present. Paulette Bodeman offers readers "her story" without any glossy finish, soft lighting, or color touch-ups. She tells of descending into the darkness, climbing (sometimes clawing) her way out, and stretching toward the light of insight and wisdom. In these pages, a reader will find connection, inspiration, and motivation.

Professor Susan Moore, English Faculty Scottsdale Community College

The BreakAway Girl

SECRETS OF A TANTRIC YOGI

Paulette Bodeman

To Julie,

May this inspire and bring support to you. Enjoy,

Paulette

The BreakAway Girl - Secrets of a Tantric Yogi

Asana and Mudra photos: Nancy Dales
Front cover and Mala photos: Kimberly Auxier Garofolo

Haikus and Poem written by Paulette Bodeman

Published January 2018

Sojourn Publishing, LLC
Sedona AZ

Paperback ISBN: 978-1-62747-221-0
Ebook ISBN: 978-1-62747-197-8

Printed in the United States

For my two Steves.

"In your vulnerable moments, you are held by the current. In your empowered moments, you swim with the current. In your ultimate moments, you and the current are one."
—Dr. Douglas Brooks

Contents

Foreword

I wasn't crazy about fish that was cooked, and this shit was *raw*. They ordered fifty pieces, all different kinds, and everybody was gobbling it. I tried one. It was tender. Sticky. Papery. Pretty good actually.

But then, that green paste. There was no way to predict the intensity. It harpooned me between the eyes. The room blurred and spun. I couldn't breathe. I thought I might die. Or worse yet, puke.

That's the last time I felt like that. Until I read this book.

I'm just giving you a heads-up. The writing is raw. It's life, the way it is. Uncooked. Ungarnished. Not served on fancy dishes.

And it's all here, all to be felt. Nothing is excluded. Not fear, or anything.

In one of his poems, Raymond Carver says, "Put it all in. Make use." That's what Paulette has done. She's included everything, and made good use of it.

It takes guts to write a book like this. Even to read it. To stay with it, not knowing what's next, and let yourself be affected.

Life gives us plenty of raw material. Sometimes more than we think we can stomach. But, as Paulette demonstrates, it's all workable.

—Steve Price, Personal Coach, Yoga teacher trainer and published author of seven books

Dear Reader,

When I began writing this book, I wasn't sure why. Except that pieces and parts of myself have been calling out to me for a very long time.

I shoved the words back into the cave of my mind, only for whole paragraphs to rise up at the oddest moments. Like when I'm making love. Praying. Or flossing my teeth.

I hid them in the closet. An image poked its head out, leering, "Remember me?"

The thing is, if I didn't excavate this inner quarry, I wouldn't be fulfilling my agreement with that intangible something, or someone. The one who continued to poke a finger at my shoulder. Prodding, "Come on. Get going."

If I kept turning my back on this vague specter, the part of my essence that longs for expression, it would eventually leave me. Alone. Abandoned. Like past lovers. I'd be left anxious, with a deep, un-nameable sadness.

I know, because I have tried. I know, because writing is one way I sift through the messiness of life, hoping to find a few golden nuggets.

And so, I lay my naked heart before you.

With love,
Paulette

P.S. Every day as I sat down to write this book, I committed to radical self-honesty. To not hide from my own stupidity and unskillful choice-making. Memories, though, are shape-shifters. Over time, some may take on a different guise, form, personality. Colors fade, or become more alive and vibrant. With distance, space and time, my perception of people and experiences may certainly have become shrouded in opaque recollection.

Preface

One of the main tenets of the Catholic faith is the belief in the Trinity. The Father, the Son and the Holy Spirit. In most religions, there is a reference to the number three and its symbolism of creation. In the Tantric yoga tradition that I practice and teach, there is also an association to the number three and the creation cycle.

The three masculine gods of the creation myths are Shiva, the god of dissolution and transforming darkness; Brahma, the emanating force of creation; and Vishnu, who sustains and maintains the physical form and gives the appearance of stability.

For me, especially as a woman, I'm drawn to the archetypes of the three feminine goddesses: Kali, Saraswati and Lakshmi, the consorts of Shiva, Brahma and Vishnu.

Kali, the goddess of darkness, is considered the mother of all. She's also recognized as the goddess of the great void. In her darkness, she contains the unlimited potential of creation. Kali is the crucible that holds your Sankalpa – the intention of your heart.

Out of Kali arises the erudite Saraswati. The goddess of sequence and flow. She's the embodiment of the arts. Knowledge. Speech. Wisdom. Saraswati is the goddess we call upon to assist us in any creative endeavor. As the goddess of Krama Shakti or divine timing, Saraswati gives wings to your Sankalpa in order for it to set sail.

From the depths of Saraswati arises the goddess Lakshmi, the goddess of purnatva or fullness. Fullness in this sense of the word implies richness, which is radiant with vitality, lushness and abundance. When we awaken and appreciate the boon or gift that is our life, we manifest our heart's desire and actualize Lakshmi.

What is important to note is that the sequence of the goddesses may vary between traditions. However, most lineages would agree that all three goddesses exist within us simultaneously – equal in their power and their presence, one within the other – whether we are female or male. In our humanness, we separate them out in order to understand the contributions that they offer, and how we might call upon these aspects of self when we are in need of the support they symbolize.

It is in their honor that I have written this book in four parts – beginning and ending with Kali – as this is how the goddesses arose in my life and in my recognition.

Part One – Kali. For what appeared to be a dark time in my life, the reality is, I was always supported by Kali's loving grace and the power of potential for the light of my heart to shine through.

Part Two – Saraswati. As life unfolds in her divine timing, this period brought me to the place of developing a deeper relationship with my inner being and wisdom.

Part Three – Lakshmi. At this particular stage, I'm grateful for the ability to appreciate the rich tapestry of the life I have woven together, with golden threads of love and joy as well as the seemingly discolored. They are all threads of the goddess weaving through life. Mine. And yours.

Part Four – Kali. As the great mother, everything begins and ends with Kali. She is the spark that ignites life itself. And to her do we return. As we dissolve back into the subtle void of potentiality, we are liberated.

KALI
Part One

"Seeds of Love We Plant
It is the Highest Teaching
From the Muck We Bloom"

Chapter One
~~*Brown Eyed Girl Gone Bad*~~

My client arrives early for his standing every-other-week 4:00 pm appointment. Shampoo, trim and blow dry. Fifty-five years old, slim, dapper, silver-gray hair. Glacier-blue eyes gaze directly into mine.

He hands me a flier. "Take a look at this. I've been hearing a lot about how yoga and meditation can help people with stress refocus their thoughts and generally feel better. It's probably none of my business, but I don't think I've ever seen you without a cigarette dangling out the corner of your mouth. Who knows what else you're smoking? The dark circles under your eyes look like bruises. I'm worried about you."

~

It's 7:00 pm on a five-degree Chicago winter evening. My car heater blasts warm air but I still see my breath. I pick up the yoga/meditation flyer lying on the passenger seat. Yep, this is the place. As I open the car door, the icy wind blowing off Lake Michigan steals my breath.

Fighting the wind, I run across the parking lot to the front door. Hesitating, I walk in.

A tall woman dressed in white, flowing garments with a white turban wrapped around her head stands just inside the entryway. The room is fragrant with incense. Instantly, I'm transported to Sunday morning mass – air heavy with the swirl of frankincense.

My eyes dart back and forth. Ten rows of burgundy seat pillows fill the room. Like a frightened animal, I search for an easy escape. Too late. Turban Woman smiles and guides me to one of the few unoccupied cushions in the back row.

The room is silent. I'm certain everyone can hear fear thumping loudly against my breast. Unlike church, where a priest stands commandingly at the front of the room, three large photographs of Indian men are prominently positioned instead.

Seated, I huddle inside my bulky down winter coat. Suddenly the room comes alive with the sound of singing. What I hear is a jumble of sounds. I have no idea what they mean. Oddly, I feel comforted. The singing picks up speed, volume and intensity. Then just as abruptly as it began, it stops.

Silence. No human movement stirs the air. Only the lingering waft of incense. I open my eyes to see what's going on. Nothing. People are sitting tall and erect with their eyes closed. I'm a peeping Tom. I close my eyes again for what must be hours. It's only thirty minutes.

I return the following week, and the following week, and then the next. A foreigner visiting another country. Some weeks, Turban Woman and two of her friends lead us in stretches. I buy a yoga mat. So, this is it, I think. "This is yoga."

I roam the bookstore, purchasing book after book with my weekly haircutting tips. Many of them have strange names and authors. *Autobiography of a Yogi. The Bhagavad Gita. Patanjali's Yoga Sutras. Richard Hittleman's Yoga: 28 Day Exercise Plan.*

Trembling. Shaking voice. I ask questions when sitting in circle during Q and A night at the ashram (yoga and meditation center). Who knows? Maybe this thing called yoga will save my life.

~

In the corner of my bedroom, I set up an altar. Reverently, I place a framed black-and-white photo of my late grandmother. She's wearing a scoop-neck silk dress. Fabric roses attach to the gathered waistline. Sequins run through the skirt, giving it a little sparkle. Her long brown hair, pulled back into a bun, shows off dangling pearl earrings. A quiet little smile plays at her lips. She looks straight into the camera. What is she really seeing?

Setting my kitchen timer for fifteen minutes, I take a seat on my hardly-broken-in meditation cushion. I stare back at my grandmother.

~

She steps off the bus carrying a linen grocery bag filled with long, thin string beans. Deep purple eggplants. Red and green tomatoes from her garden. As I run to her, she sets down her bag and wraps warm, plump arms that smell yeasty like the homemade bread she lovingly baked for us. Grabbing my face in her hands, she kisses me on both cheeks the way they do in her native Italy.

Hand in hand, we walk the six blocks to back to the apartment. Our overweight Chihuahua keeps time alongside us, dragging his right hind leg. We never walked him on a leash. Just opened the back door when he needed to go out and he'd return anywhere between ten and fifteen minutes later. One afternoon we heard a car screeching and a wail that sounded like a baby's scream.

And there he was, flung to the side of the street with a broken leg. He wore a cast for weeks, but that leg never did heal right.

My grandmother walked slowly, which made it easier for the dog to keep up. She was not only burdened with the fruits of her labor, but from her bulky, black, mannish-looking shoes. Heavy, thick stockings. Black mourning dress (donned years past when her son was killed) and black shawl covering her shoulders – regardless of the temperature.

Every now and then as we strolled home, her rapid-fire Italian burst through with a heavily accented English word. Just enough so that I followed the thread of her conversation.

I sit next to my grandmother at the kitchen table and help her snap the tips off the earthy green beans. My mom speaks in the reverse of her mother. Mostly English with an Italian word thrown in every once in a while. They laugh a lot. I watch. Snap. Listen.

~

My third-grade teacher is Miss Slater. She wears suits to school. Little jackets with starched white blouses underneath, and pencil-thin skirts. Her short, reddish-brown hair is styled in a perfect bouffant bubble. Tortoiseshell glasses make her seem smart and wise. I'm infatuated. Someday I'll be a third-grade teacher.

~

A scream pierces my sleep. I glance at the clock. 9:00 am. I'm late for school. How come no one woke me up? What will Ms. Slater think? Running to the sound of my mother's crying, I find her and my father sitting on their rumpled bed. My father looks up from stroking her back. His eyes are bloodshot. Teary.

I freeze. If I hold my breath long enough, I'll be sitting at my desk in school.

My mother raises her head and opens her arms to me. Feet Velcroed to the floor, I'm immovable. She drops her arms, and with the back of her shaking hand, wipes the tears. Choking, I can barely hear her.

"Honey, Grandma died."

~

"Fuck it! This shit is too hard." I throw all of my new books into an old packing box. Shove the meditation cushion in last. Dump them in the basement storage shed. I never step foot inside that ashram again.

~

When I was six years old, I hated playing with dolls. They were a waste of time. Then my youngest brother was born. Perfection. A living porcelain doll. Round, shiny pink cheeks and forehead. Tiny red goldfish mouth. A thicket of black hair. Fairy ears. Long, slender fingers and teeny nails. Sitting on our yellow velour sofa, my mother places him in my arms.

"Thanks, Mom. Is he mine?"

"Well, no, Honey. He's your little brother. He doesn't belong only to you. He's part of the family now."

"No, you're wrong. He's mine."

~

I couldn't get enough of him. Even changing his diaper was not a chore. My mother taught me how to push the pins in just so, in order to not stick his soft little body. Then I'd dress him up, place him carefully in the brand-new red plaid buggy and parade him up and down the street. Well, I was only allowed to walk three houses in each direction. But it was the grandest of strolls along a fancy promenade.

~

Today is my birthday. Christmas Eve.

We're sitting around the dining room table. Me, the baby who is now eighteen, my mother, father, and my best friend, whose husband recently walked out on her.

My brother leaves the room and returns with a cake lit up with sparkling birthday candles. He places it in the center of the table, and they begin to sing. I hear my brother only, as he chants, "Sad birthday to you, sad birthday to you, sad birthday Paulette, sad birthday to you."

I am lost in space.

~

The alarm buzzes. No need. I'm a zombie. I stumble to the bathroom. Flip the switch. The fluorescent light casts a sickly, muddy tinge to the small room. I look in the mirror. Hair limp. Straight. Dirty. My shade stares back at me. Red-rimmed eyes, pupils unusually large, skin greenish-gray. Mouth a cavern of dirty sand. I unscrew the plastic bottle of Listerine. Swish gargle swish. I want to vomit. I detest vomiting. So, I don't.

The shower water almost blisters my skin. Just the way I like it. I turn the handle to cold.

Wiping the mirror with the edge of the bath towel, I look into it again. "Who the hell are you?"

My trembling hands pour a cup of coffee. Bile chars my throat. I eat a cracker. I'm a rabbit, nibbling one teeny bite at a time. I keep it down. Through the fog, "If you were pregnant, you'd probably be feeling nauseous. Eating a cracker." I'm not pregnant. Not single. Not married.

Pulled back into the bathroom, I speak out loud. My voice distorted. "Mirror mirror on the wall, am I a freakin' druggy?"

~

My best friend drags me to a therapist. I pretend the three of us are going to have "girl time." But it's not a social visit.

She wraps her arms around me, "You have to do this. You know that, don't you?"

I hug her back but don't answer. She gives me a shove, and I walk into the office alone.

The therapist rips my guts out. I love/hate the sessions. They are forcing me to get real. A chance that I can piece my shattered Humpty Dumpty self back together again. It sucks looking at those demons staring back at me. Shaking and scared, I dive into Hell, determined to face my brokenness.

In the late hours of the night, my mind bumps up against a threshold. *Is that what yoga was offering you? Courage to look inside? Why'd you run?*

I no longer need my best friend to escort me by the hand to therapy. I walk in solo and settle into a cushy wingback side chair. I imagine it was chosen just so that wound-up, twisted people like me might relax, and puke out their tainted leftovers.

The therapist towers over me. She's maybe five foot ten. I desperately want to ask her exactly how tall she is. But even in my fuzzy state, I know that to be rude. For just the opposite reason, at all of my five foot one, I hate it when people ask me, "So are you even five feet?" patting me on the head as if I were a cartoon character.

She wears her hair short and dyes it carrot red. Her voice is soothing, though every now and then she stutters and her questions end on a high note.

"Paulette, do you remember when you began to experience anxiety?"

"Yeah... the night he left me."

~

I'm sitting on the floor in the living room, wrapping presents. Red, green, gold, silver bows and strewn paper. My rhythm syncs to Van Morrison wailing *Brown Eyed Girl*. Reaching for the scissors and tape, I detect him standing in the doorway. Still. Silent. He stares.

"Jesus Christ, you scared the hell out of me."

Nothing. Just that stare.

My heart stops. Then it starts again. Thrashing. A pummeling against the inside of my chest. My breath in short gasps. Scissors and tape slide from my sweaty palms. The pounding in my ears drowns out the music.

His face like melting wax. "Paul, I don't think I want to be married anymore."

My question a slash. "What are you talking about?"

"I don't know. I just feel... I mean. We've been together so long. Since we were kids. I don't know how to be me without you."

"Yeah, so? That's what being married is all about. You're together."

"Paul. I'm sorry. I just gotta be me."

~

I was never athletic like my three brothers. They played softball and street hockey, ran track, and Middle Brother, well, he rode a shiny red minibike all over the neighborhood. Jamming the gears so hard he'd whiz by like a vision.

Oddly enough, what I did like to do was run. I'd put on my worn-out, fishy-smelling Keds and take off. The feel of my heart pumping in rhythm with my legs, and the steady swing of my arms, were marvelous.

I'd run north one block on Nordica Avenue, cross over Diversey, then another five blocks to my best friend's house. Other times I ran without destination or route.

Just me and my feet slapping against the pavement, stomping out all thoughts.

Sometimes after school, we ran relay races at Reese Park. Just for fun. No one really cared who won. But maybe because of the way I was built – small, thin and wiry – I won a lot.

Then one day, riding up on his silver-gray Schwinn Stingray bike, he showed up as if he belonged. As if he were already one of us.

My cousin calls me over. "Hey Paulette, I think we found someone you might not be able to beat."

I turn my head slightly to the left and slyly check him out. His white T-shirt fits tightly over his chest, and dips perfectly in a V, revealing a thin gold chain with a St. Christopher's medal dangling against his dusky skin. Shirt tucked into army-green baggy pants that he's rolled up above his ankles. White athletic socks glare. In serious need of a polish – black wing-tips.

Holding out his hand he introduces himself. Coal-brown, unwavering eyes. A kick in the belly sucks the breath right out of me.

Yanking my hand back, I manage, "You want to run in those shoes?"

He nods.

Off in the distance I hear, "Come on, you guys... On your mark, get set, go..."

The kids go crazy. "He beat her! No way. Someone finally beat her!"

~

Weeks later we're riding home on our bikes. He of the silver Stingray chariot. And me on my bubblegum-pink version, with colored streamers flowing out from the hand grips.

I won that treasured bike in a contest my mother entered me in at a neighborhood shoe store, way before the days of national big-box chains. My family never wins anything. But on this day, the day we purchased my new, back-to-school penny loafers, my mother felt lucky.

We lean our Schwinns up against the side of the apartment building and plop down in the yard. I pull blades of grass and silently murmur, "He loves me, he loves me not, he loves me, he loves me not."

Lifting my chin with his soft hand, his twelve-year-old laser eyes sear. "Promise me something."

"What?"

"Promise me you'll wait for us to grow up. Because someday, I want to marry you."

Eight years later, on a cold, clear February day in Chicago, I kept my promise.

~

I'm hanging in there with the therapist. She asks me again about my birthday. A flash of lightning. A connection.

"You know, my mother had a sad birthday too."

"Tell me about it?"

~

I spy my mother as she lightly strides across the length of our kitchen. Talking, laughing, stretching the coiled wall-phone cord as far as it allows. Then she pirouettes like a ballet dancer, gliding back to where she started. My mother smiles. Radiating delight. Hanging up the phone she turns, wrapping her Chanel #5 arms around me. Her love fragrant.

"Mom, you look beautiful."

Her naturally dark-brown hair has been lightened to the color of summer wheat. It's twisted and pinned up to show off her long, slender neck, where the pearls that were my once my grandmother's lay perfectly above her collar bone.

They're not expensive pearls. Maybe even imitation. But against the smoothness of my mother's tender neck, they are luminescent.

In her black stiletto heels, she stands a regal five foot two. The silkiness of her shimmering evening dress drapes her small frame perfectly.

She's taken extra care with her makeup. Curled blackened lashes frame her hooded eyelids. They're outlined in a deep, rich cocoa-brown pencil, matching the color of her eyes.

I'm mesmerized. Will I ever be as lovely, elegant, entrancing? Today my mother is Queen.

"Where're you going tonight to celebrate?"

"Dad's taking me to our favorite steak house. You know, the one with the piano bar. I'm sure he's arranged with the piano player so that he can sing *Happy Birthday* to me. He'll want to surprise me, but it's tradition now. So, I'll play along to humor him."

"Does it still make you happy, Mom?"

"Of course it does. Now finish up your homework so you can keep an eye on the boys tonight. I'll let you know when we leave."

My bedroom is right off the kitchen. Closing the door behind me, I focus on math and English. A shriek shatters the silence. Sobbing. Deep, sick-to-your-stomach wailing.

I fling the door open. My mother lies crumpled on the floor of the kitchen, rocking. Rocking back and forth, the phone cradled against her breast.

"Mom! What is it? What's wrong?"

She doesn't answer me. I'm not even sure she knows I'm there. Dropping to my knees, I place my hand to her shoulder. "Mom, what's going on?"

My mother lifts her head, eyes unfocused, and tries to speak, but no words come out. Mascara runs in rivulets down her cheeks, while her perfectly applied makeup now smears her face clownishly. Her soft, loving eyes are swollen, red, scared, angry.

"Mom, listen to me!" I yell at her. "Who just called? Tell me what's happened."

"I think your dad is having an affair."

~

My best friend and I join a gym. It's for women only. I can't bear to be around a gym full of sweaty, hard-bodied men. We meet up twice a week and lift weights. Walk the treadmill. Take a yoga class. It's something to do. And then we go out to dinner.

Walking to our cars, I stop. Fish around in my purse and pull out a lighter and pack of Winstons. I take a long drag and slowly exhale the smoke into the night.

My friend faces off with me. "Are you kidding me?"

"What?"

"You know what. We just worked our butts off, and the first thing you do is light up that damn cancer stick!"

"I know. I know. I'm gonna quit."

"I've heard that before."

"Come on. Cut me some slack. Some habits are hard to break."

~

It's Saturday night. We're having a date night. I open the door to my limbo husband. An Al Pacino/Serpico lookalike.

Vigilantly he stands. Maybe five foot eight or nine-ish. Dark-brown, almost black hair grown over his ears, touching his collar. Luscious red lips the star of his full beard. Oversized tinted glasses unable to hide long lashes and almond-shaped eyes that burn.

Opening the door wider, I try not to fling myself at him. He leans towards me, going in for a kiss. Quickly I spin around and stride into the living room.

"Come on in," I toss over my shoulder.

Looking through the entry, he says, "Nice. It looks like you. You happy here?"

I glare at him. "Happy?"

He perches on the couch. I sit across from him on my new, canary-yellow reading chair. Gripping the slender cane arms, I settle back.

From the pocket of his brown leather jacket, he pulls out a pack of Marlboros. "Can I smoke?"

"I'd rather you didn't. I quit."

"Good for you."

He sounds surprised. Suspect. Or maybe it's my imagination.

He asks to see the rest of my condo. Pausing in the narrow hallway, he gazes at the perfectly lined framed photos of the Roman Colosseum.

"You took those last summer?"

"Yeah."

"They're good."

We walk back to the living room and assume our positions. Reaching into his pocket again, he pulls out a square of tin foil. Carefully he opens the edges, licks his index finger, dips it into the white powdered gold. Leaning forward, he swipes it across my bottom lip.

Then, like magic, a crisp $100 bill materializes in his hand. Precisely, tightly he rolls it.

Casually he looks up at me. "You got a razor and a mirror?"

~

We're twin octopuses. Tentacles entwined round each other. Whose appendage belongs to whom? Releasing one, another wraps itself tighter. I'm drowning at the bottom of the sea.

~

My baby brother calls, informing me he's taking a trip to Mexico with my almost-ex-husband.

"Are you nuts?"

"No. I'm not. Just listen."

"Listen. To what? You of all people. I can't believe you're doing this to me."

"I'm not doing anything to you. Hey, you brought him into our lives. We've been friends for years."

"Now you have to do this? The timing is a little suspicious. Whose idea was it anyway?"

"His."

"Of course it was. Jesus. Go... Go. And I don't want to hear anything about it."

"You know you still love him."

"No shit."

~

My almost-ex, almost dies. Three days into vacation he's either retching into the toilet bowl or sitting on it. A Mexican doctor prescribes pills. He rallies for a few days. Returns home. Returns to work. The parasite bides its time.

He's hospitalized. For weeks, the doctors are unable to determine the type of freeloader organism it is. His voice barely recognizable, he begs me to visit.

I walk through the door.

Weak, thin, hollowed cheeks. Eyes dull. His smile struggles. I want to be anywhere but in this room. We stare at one another. He barely lifts his hand. I pull the chair close to the bed. His ragged breath frightens me. I lay my face to his forehead. A four-alarm fire. Hands clammy cold. I don't know if he's trembling because I'm there or because he's really, really sick.

"I love you."

"Shh... not now. It's okay. You need to get better."

A tentacle tightens.

~

I run to the phone.

Hand shaking, I answer. "Hello." Silence. Then, "Paul, I want to come home."

It's 3:00 am. We're in bed. Two molded spoons. Legs entwined. His breath whispers at the back of my neck. I listen to his soft snoring.

How many women has he been with? Do I know them?

Carefully I untangle myself, slip out of bed, throw on a pair of sweats and pad downstairs to the kitchen.

Finding a pen, I write. "My heart feels like one of your worn-out racquetballs smashed against an indifferent concrete wall. I can't play this game any longer."

Like a cat burglar, I sneak back up the stairs. I reach out to touch him. Instead, I place the note in the still-warm impression of my body.

The back door groans as I close it behind me.

Chapter Two
~~*I'm A Nordica Kid*~~

That's what we call ourselves. "The Nordica Kids." We say it with aplomb. As if the eight of us share a secret. I have one older brother and two younger. We live in a two-flat. Though really, I think it's one of the first condominiums built in the Chicago area. Right here on Nordica Avenue.

We aren't considered true city dwellers. Yet we don't live in the suburbs. I imagine Nordica Avenue is a tract of land that's neither here nor there. Our own little Shangri-La.

~

My four cousins live upstairs. The twins are six years older than me. I follow them around until they shoo me away. Annoyed. They play the piano and their favorite song is *Copy Cat*. They have a younger brother and sister. I'm two months older than my boy cousin, and I don't know why I do it, but every chance I get, I bite him. I don't mean to hurt him. He's just so bite-able.

My grandparents were supposed to live in the garden apartment. A fancier word than basement. But when it got right down to it, they wouldn't budge. So, our parents rented it out to a young newlywed couple.

During sex, they moan so loud we hear it in our apartment. My brothers think it's hysterical. I flush with shameful curiosity. After two years of sex education from the renters, they divorce, leaving the apartment empty, echoing love turned sour.

My mom and dad run a tight ship. Like most of the kids in our neighborhood, we have a set bedtime. Eat dinner regularly together, and pick up our dirty underwear off the floor.

Every Saturday I help my mother clean the apartment. "From top to bottom." One of my tasks is to carry a metal bucket filled with warm water and foaming with Pine Sol. I try not to gag. Every single wooden window sill in the apartment is wiped down, scrutiny-ready. Just like the postal service. "Neither snow nor rain nor heat nor gloom of night stay these couriers from the swift completion of their appointed rounds." Suffice it to say, I get the job done.

After inspection of each of my chores, my mother and I take showers, dress in matching flower-printed granny gowns and sit down to a lunch of tuna fish sandwiches on white, pasty Wonder Bread with a side of Lay's potato chips.

I have to admit that sometimes I wish I lived with my cousins. They had so much more freedom than my brothers and I did. Since our doors are never locked, I sneak up the enclosed front staircase and join the goings-on. When it's time for bed, my dad takes a broom handle and bangs the ceiling. It's either his signal for me to come on down, or a message for my cousins to cease and desist whatever fun they are up to.

My aunt's name is Ernestine. But everyone calls her Dolly. She makes dinner with a glass of Scotch in one hand, a cigarette pursed between her lips – ash dangerously threatening over the pot of simmering spaghetti sauce, and a shoulder hitched up pressing the telephone against her ear. And like my dad, boy can she vocalize. Aunt Dolly, well, she doesn't really care if the girls' dirty underwear is thrown in a heaping pile in the corner of their bedroom.

~

On the weekends, the adults like to play cards. Or they gather in our den to sing Frank Sinatra, Vic Damone, Jack Jones, Buddy Greco and an occasional token show tune.

My dad could have been a DJ. Or rather, the original Karaoke master. He has all the equipment. Racks of LPs alphabetically arranged, reel-to-reel recording tapes, a state-of-the-art stereo system with huge Bose acoustic speakers, microphones and headsets.

They sip their Manhattans or Scotches with a twist and harmonize, while we kids run up and down from one apartment to the other. When we get a little older, the boys disappear. While the girls gather in another room, our oldest cousin Florence, an honorary Nordica kid, teaches us to jitterbug. She's got all the moves down. Sometimes we put on our 45s – those small-format, one-tune-per-side circles of vinyl that we treasured – and lip-sync to the Supremes. Four little white girls impersonating the exotic Motown queens. We all want to be the sultry Diana Ross, but we agree to take turns.

~

My mom and dad, my Auntie Dolly and Uncle Rocky, they're celebrities in the hair industry. They attend conventions every year in downtown Chicago, and host competition events with the hottest up-and-coming national and international stylists. They are sought after for their charisma and talent.

The thing is, my dad doesn't really love what he does for employment. He's more of an introvert. Hairstyling is merely a profession, and a means to an end. He earns a good living that supports his family. My mom – she's in it for a host of other reasons. To keep a handle on the finances, because that's not my dad's thing. To stay in touch with what's happening in my dad's world (something she learned after the long-ago birthday fiasco). And to build my father up. He's not as tough, secure or confident as he appears. They make a good team.

My uncle, on the other hand, is all about the showmanship. He thrives on the attention and notoriety. Plus, he enjoys everything about the hair industry. He's good at it. My aunt, she's more in line with my mother's objectives. Yet she fits her name – she's our own version of *Hello Dolly,* or better yet, Auntie Mame. She's fun. She makes you laugh. Sings like a jaybird. Loves people and socializing. While they too make a good team, the problem is, my aunt and uncle don't always see eye to eye.

My uncle likes to take off. Some days, we don't know where he is. The stylists who work for him call my aunt to see why he hasn't shown up at the salon. He has a line of clients waiting.

A few years later, the twins are groomed for the business. They're over-the-top talented. The two of them win more awards than my dad and uncle combined. So, now they work in the salon and have to field the recurring query, "Where's Rocky?"

On one of those disappearing days, just by chance, we learn that he's hopped a plane to Vegas.

The little problem my aunt and uncle have is that Rocky likes to gamble. We also learn he stays at his hotel of choice, The Stardust. Rocky even has a favorite room. The good news is that once that's established, the family knows where to find him. The bad news: How much money was he going to lose?

My Uncle Rocky – nobody can stay angry with him. Even the people he owes money to. They know that ultimately, they'll get it back. I don't know how he manages it, but he does.

His smile curls up like Elvis's and his blue eyes are as startling as Paul Newman's. I love him as much as I love my aunt.

~

At least once a week, Rocky climbs the back stairs and peeks in our kitchen window. If we're sitting down to dinner, he taps the window with his pinky ring, walks right in and picks up the conversation he started the week before. His favorite thing is to trick me to look away, grab something off my plate and pop it into his mouth. I pretend not to catch on, so that he'll keep doing it.

My mom and my dad, on the nights he makes it home for dinner, try to direct the conversation to how Rocky is doing; what's going on, money, bills. They own the apartment building jointly. The four of them are in this venture together. But Rocky's purpose is always family connection. No discussing serious issues. Ever. My uncle, he's like the wind.

He stays for a few minutes. Lights up our kitchen like only he can. Then kisses me on the cheek. Calls me Pauletina. Dips a piece of crusty bread into my bowl of pasta with meat sauce, waves it in the air and announces, "Okay, time for me to head upstairs and get my medicine."

I was never sure if his medicine was his companionable Scotch with my aunt. Or her wrath. Or a little of both. That's the conundrum of Rocky and Dolly.

~

I'm thirteen when I beg my mother to let me get my ears pierced. She's not thrilled. I remind her that we're Italian after all, and in Italy, infant girls have their ears pierced within hours of being born. She retorts that we're not in Italy.

"But the twins have pierced ears. And Auntie Dolly will pierce them for me. It won't cost a red cent. All we need is a pair of earrings."

Finally, she relents.

After dinner, I run upstairs for the big event, where my aunt and cousins are anxiously waiting. It'll be a breeze, they assure me. One, two, three, and it's over.

I haven't told you yet, but I'm known as the Scaredy Cat of Nordica Avenue.

~

Most times, my words get stuck in the tunnel of my throat. They long to rise up and out. But I'm so tense with fright. If I let the words loose and they flow, like a babbling brook, I'll never be able to stop them. So, I seal the words inside, much like putting a cork in a bottle.

Though my words, they never truly die. They just sit there, impatiently waiting. Hot and moist, they travel down into the pit of my stomach. Every once in a while, I feel armed, like when I have my favorite, Sunday-labeled panties on. Determined, I slowly set a few words free.

If you asked me what exactly I'm afraid of, I would begin to list the usual offenders. Snakes. Spiders. Noises in the night. Rapists and murderers. A nuclear war with Russia. Stepping on a sidewalk crack. Learning how to drive. Growing up. Going away to college. Getting my ears pierced and so on....

~

"Come on, Pauletina," my Uncle Rocky's favorite idiom for me. "It will only hurt for a minute," as he lifts me up onto the kitchen counter.

The twins each hand me an ice cube wrapped in a wet paper towel to hold against the front and back of each ear. Waiting for my ears to numb, my aunt pours herself a second, or possibly a third, shot of Cutty Sark. If I ask really nice, maybe she just might share a slug.

Ice cube-numbed only, I jump off the counter, proudly studded.

~

Right about the time of the ear-piercing extravaganza, my mother takes me for my first gynecology appointment. I've been having some issues.

The doctor is Chinese and speaks with a heavy accent. She turns away from me, while I'm still lying on the examination table, and blandly speaks as though she's reporting weather conditions.

"Daughter has infantile womb. She have hard time pregnancy. May never have child."

I shoot up like a rocket and pull on my panties.

"What did she just say? I'm gonna have a hard time having a baby?"

I'm a little freaked. But I'm only a kid, so I figure, well, that's stupid. Of course, my insides are small.

Though even today, all these years later when I least expect it, I walk into a doctor's office, and the smell of impending sadness slaps me in the face.

~

Every three months, my mother piles us into her yellow convertible Pontiac Catalina and drives fifty minutes to my dad's hair salon. The clients ooh and ahh over how cute we are.

Middle Brother stands out from me and Number One Brother (the baby isn't born yet). With his white-blonde hair and deep, deep brown eyes, there's just something about him that compels people to reach out, unbidden, and touch him. Especially his silken hair. He, on the other hand, cringes.

My mother dresses him in cute little outfits, with caps to match. Without fail, on the ride home, he opens the back window and tosses his hat to the wind. I often wonder if he's trying to tell her something.

When he's about six or seven, he conjures up an imaginary friend named Billy. Middle Brother and Billy are best buds. Billy is always, and I mean always, getting blamed for my brother's misadventures. At first, I think it's cute. Now, I'm fed up.

There's a new house going up on the corner of our block. We aren't allowed anywhere near the construction site. With loose boards, nails lying around, and unsavory laborers, goodness knows what might happen.

My mom is fixing dinner. I'm delegated to peeling potatoes. Billy's best friend, my brother, sneaks in the back door like a thief. But my mother's extra-sensory perception can feel him minutes before he slides in. She's ready for him.

Without even turning from the stove she smoothly demands, "Didn't I tell you to stay away from the construction site?"

He doesn't flinch. "I wasn't there."

"Oh no? Well Chris next door told me he saw you. And, he told you to get on home immediately. You ignored him."

"I didn't see Chris. It wasn't me."

"Are you telling me Chris is lying?"

"No, I'm not saying that. It just wasn't me."

"Then who was it?"

"It must've been Billy."

My mother turns around, opens her arms, pulls him in and whispers, "I don't want you going anywhere near that site. It's dangerous."

"I know, Mom. I promise. I'll tell Billy not to go there, too."

Like dynamite, I explode. "There's no such thing as Billy! For crying out loud, how long are you going to let him get away with this? I can't take it anymore."

Yet, all I do is pick up another potato.

~

I'm in my bedroom with the door closed. There's shouting in the kitchen. I put a cup against the door. My ear to the cup.

"I'm telling you there is something wrong with that baby!"

My dad sounds angry. He's not. He's worried.

Our baby cousin is eighteen months old. The doctor reports she has colic. When she's not crying, her face is the sweetest I've ever seen. But she cries more and more every day.

My dad flings open the kitchen door. He storms out. Stomps up the back stairs. Doesn't even knock. Just steps right into my aunt and uncle's apartment. With both back doors open, I don't need a cup.

"That baby is sick. She's burning up with fever. If you don't take her to the hospital now, I will."

The phone rings. My mom answers. Crying, she hands the phone to my dad. Tears stream down his face. He slams the phone on its hook. Then bashes his fist into the wall. The baby has spinal meningitis. My mother drives to the hospital. My father stays home with us kids.

"Go upstairs and get your cousins. Tell them to bring their rosaries and meet me in the living room."

My dad tries not to frighten us. He explains that our sweet little cousin is very sick. She and the doctors need our prayers. He has us form a circle on our knees and together we pray the rosary.

Ironically, it happens to be the feast of Saint Rocco. My Uncle Rocky, my mother's brother, is the baby's father. A statue of Saint Rocco is paraded through the streets in a long procession. People pray, cry and offer donations on behalf of their loved ones. Several aunts and uncles attend the feast of Saint Rocco for my cousin. They walk, pray, and pin money to the statue, bartering with God to save her life.

~

Now just the other day, I'm talking to my all-grown-up and married baby cousin. She has recently learned that those same aunts and uncles donated their wedding rings on her behalf. My cousin researches and finds a Catholic community in her area that continues to honor the feast of Saint Rocco. She's so moved by this news that she and her husband have decided to donate their wedding rings, in deference to the deceased relatives who begged God for her life.

~

It's the Fourth of July, and one of the twins is getting married. My three brothers and I are in the wedding party. My cousin has been dreaming of this day since she was a little girl.

The room is decorated in red, white and blue. The master of ceremonies announces each couple by name, and we in the wedding party strut proudly, holding holiday sparklers. I'm a supporting actor in my cousin's Italian-American version of a Bollywood film production.

A twenty-piece live band plays disco music and Sinatra tunes. My aunt, the mother of the bride, and my dad, join the band on stage and sing as if they were superstars. I guess they are.

I'm slow-dancing with my boyfriend when my mother pulls at my arm. "I can't find your brother." She sounds scared. "Have you seen him?"

"Mom. I have three; which brother?"

I look at her face. A punch in my stomach, I know who she means. Middle Brother.

"Don't worry, Mom, we'll find him."

My boyfriend and I make our way off the dance floor to one of the two bars. I squeeze his hand. "Oh, my God."

My ten-year-old brother, who doesn't stand tall enough to even reach the bar, is leaning up against the wall with a drink in his hand. We walk towards him. Like a jester, he smiles foolishly.

"What do you think you're doing? Who gave you this drink? How many have you had?"

He can't speak. He can't walk. My boyfriend and I each grab him by an arm and half-carry, half-drag him out of the ballroom.

~

Our apartment is long and narrow. Three bedrooms line against one side. Because I'm the only girl, I get a bedroom to myself. My parents another. The three boys share the last bedroom. It's crowded. Noisy. Smelly.

Middle Brother likes his space. So, my dad takes the room in the basement, which was built to be a wine cellar for my grandfather, and converts it into a bedroom.

He cuts a hole in the floor of the den, and installs a circular, wrought-iron staircase that leads down into Middle Brother's brand-new private abode. My brother puts up rock star posters and a black light.

Sometimes he invites me down, and we sit on his futon listening to music with headphones. Pink Floyd, Led Zeppelin, Fleetwood Mac, The Stones, and my favorite, Uriah Heep.

Late one night, I can't sleep. At the top of the stairs, I call to him. "Can I come down?" No answer. "Your light's still on. Are you up?"

I quietly descend, still calling his name. Poof. Empty. The window above his bed is wide open. The screen's removed. He and Billy have vanished.

~

All of a sudden, my mom and dad, aunt and uncle, are into vitamins. They meet the president of the company and they're totally impressed with him, his product line, and the growing research substantiating the health benefits from taking nutritional supplements.

The four of them become distributors. My dad and Uncle Rocky travel to Kentucky to teach other salon owners the advantages of healthy living and the use of supplements.

They set up a product shipping and receiving department in our basement. Youngest Brother works for them part-time after school. He's lanky, thin, thirteen, and going through puberty. He's also really shy. Super smart. Youngest Brother manages the inventory and packages the product for delivery.

What we don't know, in order to stave off the onset of pimples, is that he's breaking into the inventory and mega-dosing vitamin A's like they're Tic Tacs. One day he gets sick. The next day he's not able to swing his long, skinny legs out of bed. My parents take him to the doctor. He's immediately admitted to the hospital. They run all kinds of tests. Zilch.

I sit with my mom next to his bed. Taking hold of his hand, I'm afraid his bones will shatter. My mom and I cry. Beg him to get better. We're desperate. So, we bribe him. We promise him if he gets better, the three of us will take a trip anywhere he wants to go.

We lean in close. "San Francisco."

My mom and I look at one another. Shrug. Later he tells us that visions of the Golden Gate Bridge swirled in his woozy head.

The next morning, he fesses up. The doctor confirms that yes, he's overdosed on Vitamin A. Sure enough, not a zit to be found. But the toxicology report: lethal. Severe liver damage. Weeks and weeks of treatment. Nine months later, the three of us are sitting in Alioto's restaurant on Fisherman's Wharf, dipping sourdough bread into steaming bowls of clam chowder.

~

I don't know. Middle Brother, maybe he's ten or eleven? With eight kids living in two different apartments, sometimes I get a little confused. But I do remember clearly that it's an epic Chicago snowstorm. All eight of us kids home from school. A recipe for disaster. Guaranteed.

The boys are told to clear off the sidewalks. When they're finished with that, shovel out the driveway. Then go to the neighbors.

Number One Brother lets out a yell. We all come running. He points up. Middle Brother is puffed out like the Pillsbury Doughboy in his winter garb. Smack dab on the peak of the snow-packed garage roof. He opens his arms and leaps three stories down into the snow mound piled up against the fence. He's dazed. We're all dazed. Then, like a dog, he shakes himself off. Grins. In a flash, he climbs back up to the top of the roof to do it again.

~

I live in terror twenty-four-seven. The twins call me Copycat. My brothers call me Scaredy Cat. I won't admit it, but sometimes when I'm climbing the stairs to my cousins' apartment I'm afraid to look down, in case I fall over the bannister. I look in the mirror, and I'm frightened that my right eye is smaller than my left. Maybe one day I'll wake up and my right eye will have disappeared altogether.

What really scares me (I'm afraid to even say it) is that one or both of my parents might die. And Jesus help me, if they can die, then so can I.

My dad says I'm afraid of my own shadow. What they can't understand, and truthfully neither can I, is my fascination with reading true crime novels. Truman Capote's *In Cold Blood* thrilled me for weeks.

~

Regardless of the season, I grew up sleeping with my windows open. But tonight, I feel like pushing out the walls of my bedroom just so I can breathe. It's July and we don't have air conditioning. Window fans are placed in each room. I wait until everyone goes to bed. Remove the fan. Close and lock both bedroom windows. Pull down the shades. Turn on a nightlight.

There's a mass murderer on the loose. He raped, stabbed and killed eight innocent student nurses living in a townhouse on the south side of Chicago. When I close my eyes, I see his acne-scarred face. Big, full bottom lip. Ears that flap wide.

It's 2:00 am. I hear rattling at the back door. Blood pounds my ears. I'm sure they'll burst. I tuck and roll off my bed. Slip under it.

Number One Brother flips on the kitchen light. Ransacks the fridge. Chomping on a cold fried-chicken leg, he sticks his head in my door.

"Hey, what're you doing hiding under the bed? It's hot as hell in here."

"They haven't caught him yet."

"Who?"

"Who? The killer. He could be lurking right outside for all we know."

"Oh, for Christ's sake. Besides, we're twelve feet up from the ground. What's he gonna do, climb the bricks?"

My brother sits on my bed and props a pillow behind himself.

"He can use a ladder. And by the way, where have you been so late? Mom and dad are gonna be pissed."

His left shoulder lifts to his ear. "Not if you don't tell them."

Within days, the police catch the killer. My obsession with crime novels takes a hiatus. Now, I'm into autobiographies. Sammy Davis Junior's *Yes I Can* has me spellbound. My windows remain on lockdown until winter.

~

We're warned of a blizzard. Sure enough, it comes blowing through. One bedroom window is cracked open. I climb out of bed. The sill holds four inches of snow, and I'm standing on drenched carpet. I fight with the window. Manage to get it closed.

On my way back to bed, I trip over a stool. Crash. Smash my face into a solid-mahogany bedside table. I'm stunned. I head back up to the bed and sit. I feel really weird. Wipe my hand over my face. Slick. Wet.

Turning on the bathroom light, I don't recognize myself. Blood covers my face. Drips down my chin onto the top of my pink, now brownish, flannel pajamas.

Trying not to freak out my parents, I stand at their bedroom door. I think I sound calm, cool, collected. Months later, my mother tells me that my shaking, disembodied voice was the eeriest thing they'd ever heard.

I call out softly, "Mom... Dad."

Their bedroom floods with harsh light. My mother stifles a scream.

I don't know who's asking.

"Did someone break in? Did they hurt you?" I can barely shake my head no.

"Then what happened?"

I'm senseless.

Standing in his white Fruit of the Loom briefs, my dad runs for the broom. Just loudly enough, he knocks on the ceiling. Within two minutes, our phone rings. My Aunt Dolly is the go-to pro for any and all emergencies.

We crowd into our tiny bathroom. My mother, father, aunt, and me. They clean me up and butterfly-stitch my nose with Mickey Mouse Band-Aids.

The blizzard continues to rage. Two days later, my mother follows the snowplow to the doctor's office. He commends their work. In the next breath, he informs me and my mother that I've broken my nose.

It's already not one of my finer features, and I hide my nose with my right hand on the ride home. It becomes a lifelong habit.

Six months later, I'm perched up on the bathroom countertop. Staring into the mirror, I poke around the bridge of my nose.

"Dad!" I demand. "Can you come in here?" He's heard this cry before.

"There's something in my nose. Just look at it one more time." I hand him the tweezers.

I love my father. But seeing him, I see my future. Well, let me put it this way. All my friends think he looks just like Danny Thomas.

He grabs my face with one hand and tilts it up to the fluorescent light. With his other hand, he holds the tweezers. I close my eyes. A super-quick yank. Out comes a half-inch sliver of mahogany nightstand. Neither one of us speaks. Jumping off the counter, I barely make the three feet to the toilet before throwing up.

The doctor says I'm too young for rhinoplasty. "She'll have to wait until her bones stop growing."

I enter high school with a schnozz too big for my face, and a deeply etched stripe of blue/black scar running across it. The only thing that gets me to school is knowing that surgery is already scheduled three years out. Each morning with a thin, red, brand-new, just-for-this-purpose felt-tip pen, I check-mark the days off my calendar.

Chapter Three
~~*Vestal Virgin*~~

My mom and dad have come to like my boyfriend in spite of their worry about his thinly veiled machismo. Me, I'm a moth drawn to the fire. Honestly, he simmers.

They think we're too young to be getting married. Plus, they want me to go to college.

I'd be the first in the family to earn a university degree. For first-generation Italian-Americans of blue-collar immigrant parents, that would be a huge deal. My mom and dad want me to pursue my dream of becoming a teacher.

I forced myself to bury the family dream. I refocused on planning a different future. It would be *My Big Fat Italian Wedding*, with the hour-long wedding mass to be officiated at St. William's, the Catholic church we attended all through elementary school. Our wedding party made up of fourteen family and friends parading down the aisle before us. The groomsmen wearing black tuxedos, white shirts with red rosebud boutonnieres in their lapels. And the bridesmaids young and lithe in handmade burgundy velvet dresses. With the three-year-old daughter of one of the twins as the flower girl.

The reception to be held at a glitzy, brand-new ballroom, Fontana d'Or, accommodating 300 people for a sit-down dinner. With a twelve-piece live band, two bars, and a designated area just for the dessert tables and wedding cake. And to top it off, we'll head down to Mexico for a ten-day honeymoon.

Two weeks before the wedding, we're sitting on my bed, with the door open of course, when my childhood sweetheart, my soon-to-be husband, blurts out, "I'm scared, and I don't know if I can go through with this."

With one fell swoop he gutted me down the center. No words. A part of me screamed inside, *You asshole. I gave up everything for you, and now you don't know if you can go through with it?* Another part thinking, *Okay, hold on – whatever happens, you'll get through this.*

I don't know what to say or do, so I cry out, "Mom, can you come in here?"

She sends my brothers out of the house with a simple nod of her head. My father is at work, thank God. Sits us down at the kitchen table.

After a few, "How many times have I told you both that you are too damn young?" she gets it together. "Is there someone else?"

"No." I believe him; we're both virgins, for Christ's sake. At least I think he still is. Maybe that was my first mistake.

"Okay, well then. If this isn't the right time, then we'll put it off." She proceeds to walk us through how to postpone a wedding that's two weeks away.

My head spinning, I ask her if he and I can go out for a while. I've recently turned twenty-one years old, maybe getting married in two weeks, yet I still have a curfew and technically I'm a virgin.

We take a drive, and he finds a place to park in the forest preserves. It's a little creepy at night, but at least we're alone and no one will disturb us.

He pulls me to him, thrusts his tongue into my mouth and I bite down. Not too hard. Just enough.

"What the fuck!"

"Yeah, that's exactly what I'm thinking. What the fuck's going on?"

"I don't know. I'm sorry, Paul, I'm just scared I guess."

"You guess. You're the one who insisted we get married. You didn't want to wait till I finished college."

"I know. I'm sorry. I want to."

We make out for a few minutes. I pull away.

"Maybe we're just twisted up in knots with no release valve. We probably just need to do it already. I don't know why we're waiting." But we wait anyway.

The wedding goes off without a hitch. A fairytale.

~

When I least expect it, remnants of that college dream start to bubble up. I force them down with any distraction at hand. We're married. In love. Pre-jitters long gone. But sometimes I have this unsettled feeling. Like I'm just not quite right. A bit at loose ends.

"Babe, what if I went to barber school?"

He's working hard. We're socking away our savings so he can buy his own salon in a year.

"Hmm... then you can work in the shop with me. Are you sure?"

"Yes." I have to do something.

~

My best friend's having marital problems, and Middle Brother has absolutely no idea what he's going to do with his life. So, we formulate a plan. My friend and I meet at my mom and dad's house. Pick up Middle Brother and carpool to barber college. From the suburbs to the city, over an hour's drive from our meeting point. To a sketchy area of town. For maybe a year. Five days a week. Eight to five. We're in.

~

We drive round and round to find a parking space. In the cold of winter, when it gets dark at 4:30 pm. If Middle Brother isn't with us, one of the instructors walks us to our car. Out of about thirty students, there is only a handful of women. We're a new commodity in the barber industry.

Homeless people camp out in front of the barber school entryway. For twenty-five cents, they come in for a hot lather shave. Mostly, they just want to warm up. The owner of the school is kind-hearted and frequently gives the regulars odd jobs so they can get a haircut, shampoo and shave. He knows they'll use some of the money to down a drink or two.

Middle Brother always treats the homeless with humanity and dignity. In his skilled fingers, the straight-edge razor glides across those beat-up, stubbly faces as if they were to appear on the cover of *GQ Magazine*. His finesse with the blade and scissors is a surprise only to him.

Two hours every day, right before we break for lunch, we sit in a small, smelly classroom learning theory. To pass the State Boards, we not only have to give a shave and a haircut, but also pass a difficult written examination.

Most days, Middle Brother slips away during classroom hours. Sometimes he returns after lunch. When he does, I never know what shape he'll be in. I have no idea where he goes, who he's with – and what he's on.

My friend and I are worried. The owner of the school can't help Middle Brother pass the State Boards, no matter how well he wields a pair of shears. On the way to school in the mornings, we quiz him. My brother is a chameleon. His reddish-brown, shoulder-length hair, shampooed and styled, hits the top of his black wool coat as though he took a ruler and measured the space. His blue jeans are crisply ironed, with a sharp crease down the center. He's so pristine it's hard to imagine him any other way.

Test day looms near. "I'm not going to pass."

"Well, for sure you're not if you keep disappearing every day doing God knows what."

We continue to prep him for the exam.

"Okay, how many bones in the human head?"

"What's a hair follicle?"

"Short, rod-shaped bacteria are called what?"

"Promise me you'll stay in class these last few weeks."

Chapter Four
~~*Finding Jesus*~~

Middle Brother and I meet for dinner after work. Both of us are in the same business. We passed our boards, and now we're men's hairstylists working in upper-crust salons. In reality, they're just fancy barber shops. We cut, shampoo, color, blow dry and give shaves. With a straight-edge razor. He's great at it. I'm not.

It's Thanksgiving week. We both stood behind our styling chairs for thirteen solid hours. We're hungry. Tired. I really want a glass of wine. He's on the wagon, and sipping coffee, when I slide into the booth. I look at him. Who I see reflected back to me is my sweet, towheaded little brother. I order a mint tea.

He's happy. Optimistic. New job in a great salon. Making good money with generous tips. I'm hopeful. We chit-chat about clients. About the new shears, handmade from Germany, that we each purchased for $175 plus tax and shipping. Whether or not he'll come to Thanksgiving dinner with the family. And that he found Jesus.

The restaurant has an old-world feel with a tin ceiling. It's pretty. But voices bounce. Throw themselves around the room and inside my head.

"Did you just say you found Jesus?"

"Yeah."

"Well, we're Catholic. Haven't you always known Jesus?"

"No. Not like this."

"What does that mean?"

"You know how I've told you before that me and Jim Beam are best of friends."

"Yeah." I almost long for the good ol' days of Billy.

"Well." Long pause. "I ended my friendship with him. I'm done. Good news is on that exact day I asked Jesus to walk beside me. To be my new best friend."

"And?"

"He said yes."

Inhaling, I imagine I smell the oakiness and taste the black pepper, licorice, smoothness of a full-bodied Cabernet Sauvignon. I sip my tea.

He's sober. In every sense.

"That's so great. I'm happy for you." Though I don't get it at all.

We walk to our cars and wait to make sure they both start. The temperature has dropped to ten degrees below zero.

~

The speed limit on the freeway is seventy miles per hour. Forty minutes from home, I'm cruising along in the right lane, thinking about Jesus. My car jerks wildly. I'm not able to stay in the lane. The front wheels pull me to the edge. I steer left. Pulls me back and starts to slow.

I limp along on the shoulder and almost make it to the exit. Right rear flat tire. I have no idea how to change a tire. Cell phones not yet even a dream. Cars whizzing by – I'm sure I'll be killed. I get back in the car and flip on the flashers.

Five interminable minutes later, a car signals and slowly pulls up behind me. I'm afraid to get out. I unlock and re-lock my car doors. I'm looking in the rearview window, and out comes a six-foot-five, stunningly large man.

Lumbering over towards the driver's side, I slide my window down an inch. He's wearing big, heavy construction boots. A down knee-length coat. A Yukon Jack stocking cap covers his head. And a scarf wraps around his face so only his eyes are visible.

He pulls down the scarf, revealing a serious cleft lip. Pressing his face closer to the window, he speaks, but I can't hear him. A scream rises up from my belly. I push it back down. I open the window a little further.

"I know you're scared. Please don't be. I won't hurt you. Do you have a jack and a spare?"

His voice is surprisingly soft. With more than a slight lisp.

I nod yes.

"I'm gonna change the tire. First you have to pop the trunk for me."

It's frozen shut.

"Okay. I'm gonna need your keys to see if I can open the trunk manually. Now listen. I promise once I open the trunk I'll give you the keys back. Then close the window all the way. Don't be scared."

I'm living a nightmare.

It's so frickin' cold out, he struggles for ten minutes trying to unscrew the lug nuts. I wonder how he can stand it. He steps away from the car every few minutes to let me start it and run the heater.

I stop hyperventilating.

About thirty minutes later, he slams the trunk down and walks back to my window.

"You're all set. Good to go."

"I can't thank you enough. I don't know what I would have done."

My words come at him. Rapid. Staccato. Stumbling. I sound a little crazy even to my own ears.

"I have three daughters at home. I hope someone would stop and help one of them."

I pull out a twenty-dollar bill, left from my tips. Handing it to him, I start to cry.

"I wish I had more."

He refuses to accept it.

"Please. Please take it."

I push the bill through the opening.

"Happy Thanksgiving."

"You be careful now."

~

Fumbling with my house keys, I hear the phone ringing.

Middle Brother. "You promised to call when you got home. I was getting scared. What took you so long?"

"You are never gonna believe who I found on the freeway."

Chapter Five
~~*Dirty Dancing*~~

The divorce is pending. Yet here we are still playing tug of war. "Let's get back together. I really miss you." "No, I'm not ready yet."

I'm twenty-four years old. Dancing with depression. And flirting shamelessly with Black Label Scotch Whisky. On the rocks with a twist. Some days, I combine it with cocaine. My dangerous new dalliance is evidenced by my diminishing five-foot-one frame. Last check-in: eighty-seven pounds.

My family is suspicious of my extracurricular activities, but they have no solid proof. Other than me masquerading as a skeleton and behaving erratically.

I bounce a rent check, even though I have $10,000 in the bank. I make a left turn into oncoming traffic. I don't even see the car cruising towards me. I feel the impact as it pushes my Malibu sedan into a light pole. Momentarily knocked out, I come to with a stranger pounding on the driver's window, asking me if I'm okay. I don't remember where I am. I refuse to go to the hospital; the paramedics insist. Three bruised ribs. Breath capacity nil. I'm unable to work for a month.

Oh, and I'm having an affair with a coworker. He's married. I pretend he's not. The thing is – I don't even like the sex. But his face, well, he bears a strong resemblance to my absent husband. One day he tells me his wife is pregnant with their second child. I break it off. He stalks me. It goes on for months. Another game of torture.

Maybe I'm losing my mind? Maybe I'm a masochist? I call Number One Brother. Two days later, he walks into the salon, minutes before closing. Waits until every client leaves. It's only me, my brother, my stalker and my boss. I'm thinking now that maybe it wasn't a good idea I called him.

At first glance, my brother is not an imposing figure. Five foot eleven. He ran track in school. Fast. He plays the guitar and sings in a band for kicks. My brother has our father's eyes and something more. Growing up, the kids in the neighborhood called it *The Look*. If it was focused on one of them, they either took off running or hopped on their bikes faster than you can say, "Holy shit." Number One Brother. He owns it.

I touch his sleeve. "What are you doing here?"

"Go home and wait for my call."

"You're not gonna do something stupid, are you?"

Slowly. Mechanically. Out of the right corner of his mouth. "Go. Now."

~

I'm petrified to pick up the phone. I almost don't answer it. Then I make a grab for it. Neither of us says hello.

"What happened?"

"He won't be bothering you anymore."

~

My mother calls a few weeks after the car accident.

"We're taking a tour to Italy for three weeks. Come with us."

"Who else is going?"

She rat-tat-tats a bunch of names.

"I don't know anyone. Besides it's probably gonna be a lot of old people."

"You know me. Your father. Your brother. And you like old people. It's Italy for crying out loud. Not the Wisconsin State Fair."

Eight months later, we arrive in Rome. Our little band of tourists gets welcomed at The Grand Hotel. And grand it is. My spacious room on the fourth floor overlooks the Via Veneto and the Borghese Gardens.

White lace curtains blow in the morning breeze. The aroma of freshly brewed espresso and sweet-scented pastry makes me cry.

The shops along the boulevard offer luxurious goods and luscious food. Fine cashmere. Soft-to-the-touch leather bags and shoes. Linens hand-embroidered. Colorful, fragile blown glass.

Pungent aged cheeses. Briny green and black olives, dripping in extra-virgin olive oil. Wood-fired pizzas. Pasta with garlic. Lemon grilled fish.

Crunchy biscotti, Nutella-filled coronets and gelato in any flavor.

No matter the time of day the city throbs. I'm out of place. Oddly at home.

~

Our tour guide's name is Roberto. He holds a degree in Italian history. He is the opposite of my Al Pacino husband. Close to six feet tall. A little pudgy around the middle. Round cheeks. Light-brown, fine, straight hair that falls into pale-blue eyes. He smiles a lot. It probably gets him better tips. I'm not impressed.

I'm the only young woman on the trip. Another married couple brought their two teenage boys. The boys, my youngest brother and me. Everyone else – probably in their fifties and sixties. Roberto flirts. Who else can he flirt with? I ignore him. He's persistent. So am I.

On the way to visit the Catacombs, he's entertaining our little band of travelers while sharing anecdotes and pointing out historic landmarks. Lulled by the motion of the large bus, my eyes are drawn to his lips as he speaks through the microphone. Full. Red. Moist. How did I not notice? He calls me Paola.

Stepping down the stairs of the bus, after an exceptionally long day, he holds my hand longer than necessary. Bends close to my ear, inviting me to dinner.

I'm waiting outside The Grand. At 9:00 pm, the air remains heavy. Languid with the day's leftover heat. The night pulses. Music streams out of the cafes. I watch families walking together, holding hands. Teenagers preening. Lovers strolling, arms snaked around one another. Doing what lovers do everywhere. Only with more flair. They stop. Embrace. Kiss without reserve. This tradition in Italy to promenade along the boulevards at night. To see and be seen. Talk. Laugh. Discourse. Shop. Eat. Love. It's opera.

Roberto picks me up in a blue, two-seater Fiat convertible. The drive across the Tiber River is spectacular. No one obeys speed limits or traffic lights, or uses signals. Unless you count a third finger sticking straight up in the air. He slips into a parking space in a quiet, residential neighborhood. We walk half a block to the corner trattoria.

The owner greets us and guides us to a table, canopied under a jacaranda tree. Lavender petals sprinkle the tabletop. An old fisherman sits in a corner, strumming a guitar and singing softly. His skin, nut-brown like the mast of a ship deeply carved, is etched from years of exposure to the sea and sun. Every now and then the diners join in. The music and their voices grow more excited, sometimes abruptly ending in raucous laughter.

Roberto orders for us both.

While we wait for our dinner, I ask him what the old gentleman is singing about.

"Amore, of course." He laughs at my discomfort.

"All the songs are about love?"

"What else is there, Paola?"

Our dinner arrives, filling the space around us with the sharpness of garlic. Scampi drenched in olive oil. Crusty bread straight from the oven that we pull apart with our hands. The center light. Airy. It melts in our mouths. We take our time. Talk. Eat. Sip wine.

The short, squat wine tumblers remind me of my grandfather. I tell him how my mother's father made red wine in great big barrels. He drank out of a juice glass. My mother called it a magic glass, because she rarely saw it empty.

"It's good to see you eat and drink with joy, Paola. Italian women should not be so skinny."

I shake my head. "But I'm not Italian. I'm American."

"Ahh... but you're wrong, Bella."

Placing his hand on my arm, he turns it over. Gently slides his finger across the veins in my wrist.

He whispers, "Here in your blood, we are the same."

Slowly we walk back to the car. He leans up against the passenger door. Very carefully draws me to him. As if he knows I might shatter. Lightly, like a feather, he trills his lips across mine.

"We only have one night, Paola; how do you want to end it?

Chapter Six
~~*Emerging*~~

I wake from a deep sleep. Cocooned in the memory of my dream. Cloaked like the still dark night. I lean over. Turn on my bedside lamp. Reach for my journal and pen. Feeling the presence of my grandmother, I ask her to help me keep the dream close.

I'm inside a tube-like net. Though it's sticky like a spider's web. Am I the spider or the prey?

All I know is that I need to extricate myself. I look up. Down. All around. I'm in the center of a colored helix. I reach for one thread. Gently unwind and free it. The silken strands hold my DNA.

Red – fear. It's so intense my hand trembles.
Blue – shame. Stubborn it doesn't want to release. I coax it along.
Yellow – enmeshment. Where does it begin or end? For now, I leave it be.

Gray – co-dependency. It's bumped up so close to enmeshment that I'm beginning to understand.

Black – addiction. Hangs out with shame but doesn't really belong here anymore.

Orange – courage. Struggling to stand bravely for full expression.

Purple – generosity. Desires to give itself freely.

White – love. I touch it. Recognize the texture. I see its composition in the entire helix.

A velvety voice floats. "Love has the power to release and fortify."

I turn off the light. Slide the journal under my pillow. The next morning, I ransack my house. Looking for my hidey holes. First, I crush what's left of a carton of cigarettes and throw it into the trash. Then, a perfectly aged, almost-full bottle of Scotch that I pour down the kitchen sink.

Lastly, I walk into the bathroom and stare in the mirror. Making the sign of the cross, I pray out loud.

"Okay, Grandma. You've gotta help me on this one. And God, if you're really all about love, then dammit, bring it on."

I open three little packets of white powder and a nickel bag of oregano-looking green leaves. Without further ado... flush it all down the toilet.

~

My mother has a new hobby. She's into matchmaking. Funny enough, her success ratio is high. Unfortunately for me, I'm one of her favorite projects. She's determined, since I'm bankrupting her numbers. She sets me up on a blind date. The son of one of her clients. A bit risky if you ask me. But she doesn't. He's a doctor of chiropractic.

We meet at a new fondue restaurant. Order lobster, shrimp, crab, scallops, zucchini, carrots, asparagus and dip them into three different pots. Decadent pieces of fish and vegetable coated with melted cheese. Then strawberries dipped in chocolate fondue – a perfect complement to the richness of the meal.

I distract myself with the food, because I'm struggling not to stare at his hands. They are smaller than mine. *Shouldn't a chiropractor's hands be larger? They look like a child's. Only hairy. Is something wrong with them?*

We finish dinner and walk towards my car. He reaches for my swinging hand. I don't want to hold his. But I don't want to be rude. So, I let him.

My mind switches track. How I loved my ex-husband's hands. Smooth, olive skin. Long, narrow fingers. Nails clipped short and clean. Steady. Warm. Solid.

He asks if he can call. I say yes, though I know I won't go out with him again.

I open the front door. Lock it behind me. Throw down my purse and run to the bathroom. I scrub my hands until they ache.

About an hour later, I'm on the phone talking to my best friend. Telling her about the date. His hands. And my continued crazy notions – when my skin starts to itch. My face feels hot.

"I have to go. I'm feeling kind of queer."

Hanging up the phone, I walk to the hallway mirror. From underneath my skin, irregular-shaped bumps are pushing their way up. Freaky. I watch them forming. The bridge of my nose is as wide as its base. My face has ballooned to twice its size. Grotesque. I'm the main character in the movie *Altered States*.

"Mom, something's wrong with me. I'm breaking out all over my body. My eyes are swelling. I can hardly see... I'm having trouble breathing."

"We'll be right over."

The emergency room doctor asks me a bunch of questions. The words trapped. My throat is closing shut.

They shoot me full of Benadryl and pump me with Valium. I spend the night in the hospital. Diagnosis: allergic reaction to shellfish.

Are you kidding me? Shellfish. Or possibly small, hairy hands.

~

Dancing is my new drug. I float, twirl, spin. Two-step, swing and cha-cha. For the first time in a couple of years, I'm back in my body. I'm also free of it. On the dance floor, my partner is the quintessential gentleman.

He invites me to his house for a dance party. Three couples experimenting with a complex dance pattern. We laugh. Have fun. Drink wine and eat pizza. It's late. As everyone prepares to leave, he asks me to stay a moment. We sit on the couch. Discuss plans for our next dance outing.

Next thing I know, he blurts out, "I'm falling in love with you."

"No. You're not. It's just that we move well together."

"Yeah, we do. But don't you feel it too? It's more than that."

"Umm... no. I don't think so."

~

I'm staring up at his bedroom ceiling. Body numb. Mind shrieking. *What the fuck is wrong with you? Don't you know how to say no?*

Quietly I dress.

"What're you doing? It's the middle of the night."

"I have to go."

"What? Why?"

"I'm sorry. But we can't be dance partners anymore."

"I tell you I love you. You sleep with me. And now you're saying we can't even hang out together?"

"Yeah. That's exactly what I'm saying."

~

I walk through my apartment. Gaze out the front window. Barren ash trees line the stream that runs alongside the apartment complex. Gently I rub my hand over an antique roll top desk. Open the drawer and take out my trusty Paper Mate ballpoint pen. Tracing my finger over the spines of my well-stacked book shelf, I reach for my journal.

Putting the kettle on for tea, I run a bath. Add a few drops of pure essential oil into the rushing water. Lavender fills the room. I close the bathroom door. Enshrined. Drop my clothes to the floor. Slip into the water. Close my eyes. Inhale.

~

Burrowed in between pristine sheets, I write.

At first, I felt empowered by my newfound sexuality. Virgin bride no longer. In a way, I suppose, I felt I was getting back at him. Doing to him what I believe he's doing to me. The truth is, I don't know anything about him anymore. What he eats for dinner. Who his friends are. Where he spends his free time. Who he's sleeping with. All I can really know about is myself.

Who's been leading the way? What part of me is guiding my choices? My boundaries are so unclear. Muddy. Messy. Dirty.

I get out of bed. Place my teacup in the kitchen sink. Brush my teeth. Look in the mirror until I no longer can. Return to bed. Pick up my journal.

I, Paulette, commit here and now, to hold myself to a higher standard.
I pledge to respect myself and my body for the sacred temple that it is.
I vow to remain celibate until I know friendship, affection, joy and love.
Within myself. Within another.

SARASWATI
Part Two

The morning I almost died, sunlight angled through
the blinds.
The bedroom arcadia door cracked open. Jasmine
sailed on a breeze.

But wait. I must tell you that I've remarried and moved
to Arizona.

"My eyes recognize the sweetness of your smile
though we have not yet come together.
And my arms know the gentle touch of your flesh
though you have not yet lain in them.
My breasts long for the greedy suckling of your lips
though I have not yet felt such joy.
And my heart listens for the precious beating of yours
as it rests against my own.
I am waiting
for you my child
though you have not yet come to be."

Chapter Seven
~~*You Can Run,*
But You Can't Hide~~

Number One Brother is bothered by the men I'm dating. So, when he learns I'm heading south, to thaw out from wind chill temps of twenty below, he's all over it.

"I talked to my friend Steve, and he's expecting to hear from you when you get to Scottsdale. I asked him to take you to dinner."

"Really? I don't need a babysitter."

"He's not babysitting you. Steve's a good guy. I thought it would be fun for the two of you to meet."

"Sure. Okay."

~

I'm upstairs when I hear the doorbell ring.

"Come on in! Door's open! I'll be right there."

At the top of the stairs I look down.

"Hi."

"Hi. I'm Steve."

Hmm... his top lip hides behind a thick, bushy mustache. Curly, brown hair, light at the ends, encircles his head like an aura. Smiling, he reveals a crooked front tooth. He looks, well, I don't know – nice.

We're perfectly on time for our dinner reservation. A sweet, romantic place that was once a bungalow. In the former living room, now a bar, a piano player beguiles the keys.

The hostess gives Steve a hug and calls him by name. He introduces us. Then she leads us towards our table in the corner. We pause often as diners stop him to say hello.

"You know a lot of people. You must be a regular."

"Yeah. Nick is the chef and owner. The hostess – his wife. We've been friends for years. And the food is excellent."

"That's cool. What do you recommend?"

"It's hard to say. Depends on what you like. Nick's specialty is Straw and Hay. An incredible pasta dish."

We're comfortable. It feels easy. Kind of like a date. But not really.

Dessert arrives, tiramisu, the chef's favorite. Before we slide our forks in, a crash of thunder stuns us silent. Lightning slashes. Rain pounds against the front window. Waiting for the storm to subside, we sit, held in the ease of conversation.

~

The next three days are an exquisite blur.

Late one night he stirs, pulling me closer. I whisper, "Maybe you should fall in love with me."

"I already am."

~

My ex calls.

Without a breath. "I heard you were back from your trip. You stayed longer. Must have been fun. Can we meet for coffee? We really need to talk. I'm getting divorced."

Dumbfounded.

"I want to know you'll be there when I get this behind me."

A sumo wrestler sits on my chest. The kitchen fluorescent lights send shockwaves. I don't know if he's making a statement or asking me for confirmation.

Before I lose nerve, I spit out, "I'm getting married."

"What the fuck! To who?"

~

Three months later, Steve and I are on our honeymoon in San Diego, my condo is up for sale, and I wrestle free from yet another tentacle.

~

About six months into my new life, we're invited to a small dinner party. I really don't know anyone very well, but I'm comfortable. The hostess is a great cook and funny as hell. The wine flows with the conversation. After dinner, a few of us sit on the back patio. It's a typical fall Arizona evening. About sixty-two degrees and perfect for a fire in the chiminea, their tall fire-pit.

The hostess looks at me. "You want a cigarette?"

I take a drag and the smoke of my cigarette swirls with the smoke of the mesquite wood, burning in the chiminea. Just then my husband walks out. He looks at me. At the hostess. Back to me.

"I thought you quit."

"Yes, well, I did."

"But here you are. Smoking."

"Well, every once in a while, I have one."

"Then I guess you didn't quit."

I'm still learning the ways of my new husband. After all, I only knew him for three days before we decided to get married. And three months later, we were committed. Under the eyes of the Lord and the state of Illinois. I was used to Smoldering Husband. This new, reserved, white

Anglo-Saxon guy was a whole new breed. Either way, this conversation wasn't going to bode well for me.

Nothing more the rest of the night. But I could sense it. Simmering in a different way, but similar. I just never felt it quite like this before. We get in the car and silence for about ten minutes.

"You lied to me."

"Not really."

"You either lied or you didn't."

"Oh, for crying out loud. I stopped smoking and then once in a while I have a cigarette. What's the big deal?"

"For one: You didn't really quit if you're still smoking. So, it's a lie. Secondly, your Aunt Dolly. The aunt you love and have told me so much about... is dying of lung cancer. She's dying because she smoked. You hate that she's dying."

By this time, he drives into a Safeway parking lot and he's determined not to let it drop.

"So?"

He explodes. "Are you fucking kidding me?"

In a way, I'm relieved. The calm, cool and collected I don't know how to deal with. This. This I know.

"If you lie about this, what else are you willing to lie about? Your ex lied to you. It crushed you. My ex lied to me. It almost took me under. What kind of life will we have together? What kind of marriage will we have if the foundation is built on lies? It may seem a small little thing to you. But stop and think about it. It's not."

I never had another cigarette. My aunt passed away a couple of months later. Her loss broke me in ways I didn't realize it would. And while I'm not perfect, I sure as hell took those words to heart.

Chapter Eight
~~*Baby Love*~~

I've been working since I was seventeen. I'm tired. To say nothing of how I've been living the past several years. So, at first when I arrive in Arizona, all I want to do is rest.

In the mornings, I run or bike. Lie by the pool in the afternoons. Read, sleep or talk to my family and friends back home. When my husband Steve gets home from work, we cook together. Sit outside, marvel at the sunset, sip wine, eat and make love. Not bad for a Nordica kid who was running for her life in circles of stupidity.

Suddenly, a thunderbolt strikes my heart. I want a baby. WE want a baby. But guess what? Accent or not, Chinese doctor's diagnosis – affirmative. It seems that baby-making is not my forte. I wonder how that can be. In my Italian-American family, having babies is a no-brainer.

We're married about five months and I'm just not feeling well. It's probably the flu. Or maybe I'm depressed. Again.

Steve urges me to make an appointment with my new doctor.

I hand the nurse the customary urine sample. She leads me down the hall to the examining room. My doctor is a kind man who demonstrates an extraordinary bedside manner. After chit-chat and the never-not-awkwardness of a pelvic exam, I dress and meet him in his office.

A big smile beams across his face. Words escape his mouth. Bees buzz around. Lights flicker. The world hushes.

"I'm sorry. Can you say that again?"

"Congratulations. You're pregnant."

～

I'm a few minutes late for my lunch date with Steve. I rush to greet him. We hug. Kiss.

"Sorry I'm late."

"That's okay. Was traffic bad?"

I shrug and hand him a small gift bag.

"What's this?"

"Just open it."

Carefully, he reaches in and pulls out a perfect pair of white knit baby booties. My husband looks up at me. Tilts his head without speaking.

Tears messing my mascara, I nod mine in affirmation.

～

Within days, my cupcake breasts grow to melons. Loose-fitting jeans are now snug, even with the top button left undone. My heart-shaped face resembles a round globe. It's an in- and out-of-body experience at the same time. Who and what is taking over me? Keeping to my regular routine of morning runs or biking, I feel happy. Healthy.

Excited, we pack up the car and head north to Oak Creek Canyon for the weekend. To Garland's Lodge, our newly discovered hideaway in the mountains. On the drive up, Steve barely pulls off the road in time. I fling the car door open, lean my head over and throw up my breakfast of orange juice and oatmeal. Feeling better, I settle in for the remainder of the journey.

Checking into a very rustic cabin that perches over the creek, we rest before dinner in the lodge.

A fire burns in the main gathering room. Classical music softens the excited voices of the guests. Glorious smells from the kitchen tantalize. Today's menu lists many of what will become our favorites. Squash soup. Warm spinach salad, sprinkled with roasted pine nuts. Grilled salmon, drizzled in a light lemon-caper sauce. Tender baby asparagus. Truffle risotto. Warm chocolate cake dusted with cocoa.

We're seated with a husband and wife, visiting from northern California, who are celebrating their tenth wedding anniversary. Moving food around the plate, I try to disguise my growing discomfort. It's odd, because my appetite has been voracious the last few weeks. The easy banter between my husband and the other couple allows me to retreat. My inner voice screams, "What the hell is going on?"

Catching my husband's eyes, I see that I've not fooled him. Within minutes, we say goodnight. The chill of the mountain air helps revive my spirits.

Brushing my teeth, I look up into the mirror to greet my old, familiar friend named Fear. Something is not quite right. But what? I look down at my breasts. They assure me – yes, milk is filling up.

I place my hands on my expanding belly. My skin feels hot. "Please be okay, my sweet little one. I love you. Daddy and I can't wait to meet you. I want to hold you in my arms, and to feel your face against my breast."

~

Monday morning, Steve and I linger over breakfast. He kisses me goodbye, holds me tight. I stand planted in the kitchen as I listen to his car pull out of the garage and wind down the driveway. In the silence of the still house I whisper to myself, *it's going to be okay.* I don't remember how long I stood there.

Finally, I walk back down the hallway into our bedroom.

Sunlight angles through the blinds. I open the bedroom arcadia door a crack.

Piling the comforter on the floor, I yank one corner of the bedsheet off and pull. Punch. My breath short. Wrapping my arms against my middle I sit on the bed. Wait....

I stand up. Breathing's fine. That was weird. Stripping off the sheets completely, I turn to start back down the hallway that leads to the laundry room.

Jasmine floats on the morning breeze.

A sword slices through my left side. I crumple to the floor. Nauseous, I drag myself to the bathroom and heave my guts. Wiping my mouth with a bath towel, I barely make it to the toilet. My bowels erupt. I'm back on the floor, and don't know how I got there.

Somewhere in my consciousness, I know this has to do with the baby. Something is very wrong. The excruciating pain wipes out thought.

I don't know how long I lay on the cold tile bathroom floor before I crawl to the phone. Instead of calling 911, I call my husband.

Gasping between each word I manage, "You... gotta... come... home... call... doctor... the... baby. I'm... scared."

His usual half-hour commute, he makes in a record nineteen minutes. Supporting me gently, with one arm around my waist, and one hand to my elbow, he lifts me to my feet. "Steve, the baby."

Bereft of words, we shuffle to the car. My skin tissue paper is being ripped to shreds. Stopping with every other gasp, we finally make it out the front door. With gentle, loving hands, he backs me into the front seat. Lifts my legs. Places my bare feet on the floor. From a distance, I hear a scream. He tells me later it was me. Then, for a few blessed moments, I lose consciousness.

~

The emergency staff sends me directly for an ultrasound. Steve's hand is super-glued to mine. I don't know what he's whispering, but the tone of his voice won't allow me to leave my body.

I refuse to open my eyes. The doctor breaks through the haze.

Touching my shoulder, his voice sympathetic, "You've had an ectopic pregnancy. Five minutes later to the hospital... you would have died. After the ultrasound, we immediately rushed you into surgery to remove the left fallopian tube. Plus, as a result of the severe internal hemorrhaging, you needed a blood transfusion."

"But the baby... Tell me the baby is okay."

"I'm sorry. Don't you understand? You've had an ectopic pregnancy. You're really lucky to be alive."

"No, I don't! I have no idea what that means. I've never heard of an ectopic pregnancy."

"You lost the baby. I'm truly, truly sorry. You may not want to hear it now, but you're young, you're alive, you can try again."

I look at Steve. Pain. Sadness. Fear. Grief. Unable to bear it, I shut out the truth. Deliberately, I pry my hand away, and slide back down into the tunnel of darkness.

~

My new husband, of a little over a year, doesn't know what to do with me. For me. Let's face it – we hardly know each other. We met, and three months later, we got married. Chicago to Scottsdale. It seemed like a good idea at the time. Now, here we are.

He calls my mother in desperation. "She won't get out of bed. It's been three weeks. She barely eats. Won't shower. Cries incessantly. I think she's taking too many pain meds."

When my mother shows up one morning, I'm not at all surprised. She sits on the bed. Wraps her arms around me. Holds me close, expecting me to cry. But now – now I'm stone.

"It's okay. Let it go. I'm here."

The wall is impenetrable.

She makes chicken soup from scratch. Loaded with carrots, celery, turnips. I push it away. Next, she tries pasta e fagioli. Italian peasant comfort food. I swirl the spoon around the bowl.

Just the way she would with a child, she coaxes me into the shower. Helps me dress. Holds my hand and takes me for a walk. We make it about half a block. My legs are so weak, we stop to rest before turning back.

My mother is the matriarch. She can't stand that she's unable to break down the barrier. Not even a little chink.

"Don't!" I yell as she opens the blinds and arcadia door. "Close them. Please, Mom."

"Paulette. That's enough. You have to pull yourself out of this. You're not the only woman to lose a child. It's a burden we women share. Look at me."

"You didn't even want the baby you lost. So, don't tell me what I need to do." I turn away from her.

"I'm leaving tomorrow. It's up to you. Do you want to save your marriage? Or do you want it to die too?"

She's trying to shock me. Slap me into action. But I don't give a shit one way or the other.

~

The pills have vanished. So, most nights I don't sleep. I lie there and try my best not to move. Afraid that if I accidentally touch my husband, he'll think I'm turning to him for comfort. A little voice inside my head encourages me to do just that. I shut it down.

He begs me to go for counseling. I refuse. I've had enough therapy to understand what's going on. Why I'm turning my pain and grief into anger, and wearing it as a shield. And if that's not enough, like a master archer, I purposely aim my emotions at him.

Hours turn into days. Days into weeks. Weeks into months. With the intensity of the summer heat, my inner fire flares. Roars. I long to simply burn myself up on a funeral pyre.

Instead, I'm a cauldron. The Wicked Witch of the South brewing up concoctions of poison to spew.

Despite myself, as we near fall and the cooling of outside temps, my inner fire slowly begins to dampen down.

October enters quietly. I walk for hours. Along the golf course. Luscious citrus trees line the streets. I begin to recognize that even here in Arizona, there is seasonal change. Somehow that's comforting.

I don't plan it. Every day I start out on a different route. But invariably I find myself sitting on the same worn park bench. Watching the mothers talking, laughing, consoling their little children. I don't engage. I sit. Breathing. Longing.

~

It's 1:30 am. The full Hunter's Moon trickles through the slats in the bedroom blinds. I slip out of bed. Open the arcadia door. Barefoot, I step outside. My skin erupts with goose bumps in the chill of the night. Our resident great horned owl hoots and chitters from atop the chimney.

Looking up, I gaze into the expanse of the night sky. A festival of scattered diamonds. Indra's web a sparkling reflection. I am stardust.

Slowly, I roll down the waistline of my pajama bottoms, revealing a four-inch incision just above my pubic bone. It glows reddish purple in the moonlight. Closing my eyes, I glide my free hand gently, and then more firmly, across the livid, ropey scar that defines me.

When I open my eyes, I find my husband kneeling in front of me. Wrapping his arms around my waist, he pulls me close. Moves my hands away from my body. His moist lips trail along the pulsing slash of sorrow that belongs not only to me, but to both of us.

Dropping to my knees, I kiss away the tears that glisten on his unshaven cheeks. The dam breaks – flooding us with the force of our unrestrained anguish.

Soft now. Silvery we float. Feet barely touching the earth beneath, we make our way back to bed. Wrapped in stillness. No words spoken. Only the benediction of our breath. Our joining a consecration.

~

Next morning, I sit, staring into my crystal ball coffee mug. Like a disease, I feel the insidious wall of indifference building.

"Don't do it." I look up into my husband's eyes. Tenderness. A shadow of fear lurking in the corner.

He walks over to me. Cups my face in his hands. Bores into my soul. "Don't shut me out again. We can get through this. Together. But not if you keep pushing me away."

My breath syncs with the ticking heartbeat of the grandfather clock in the next room. "I've been thinking... about the therapist..."

He rushes in, "You want me to make the appointment?"
I hear the distress in his voice.
"No. No. I'll do it."

~

Circling and going nowhere. As if we're sitting in a rickety gondola on the very top of a Ferris wheel that refuses to turn. Stuck at the highest peak. Rocking in the wind.

Petrified of heights, I squeeze my eyes shut. Sweaty hands grip the handrail. My breath short. Almost panting. How did I get up here in the first place? A scream escapes. I open my eyes. It's frozen in front of me. I want to reach out and pull it back, but I'm not able to remove my hand from the rail.

~

I'm beginning to feel more solid. Steady. But still no pregnancy. I'm obsessed. Steve's terrified. Chances are higher that if I get pregnant again, I'll have another ectopic. I push that reality out of my mind.

I convince him that we should start fertility treatments. We're in the loop now. Temperature taking for scheduled sex. Neither one of us can bring ourselves to call it making love. Hormones. Drugs. Not to mention the mounting expenses we really can't afford. Our already amped-up nervous systems are nearly frayed through.

~

I'm antsy. Running isn't taking the edge off. My skin itches. My mind itches.
"What's all that?"
Spread out before me on the oak kitchen table lie catalogues for the university and the local community college.

"I picked these up at the library. I've got to do something, and I don't want to cut hair anymore. What do you think?"

"I think it's a great idea. You always wanted to be a teacher. Now's your chance. I say go for it."

"Ya know... standing behind that chair all day, for so many years, you become not only a friend, but with most clients you become a confidant. I'm thinking..."

"You're thinking what?"

"Maybe not the teaching track. Maybe counseling. I mean why not – I've done enough of it. But maybe I'm too old."

"Enough with the buts and maybes. How about thinking 'I'm taking one class and let's just see where it goes?'"

"Ha ha... I'm glad you're not just a pretty boy."

~

Today I'm at the gym, even though I hate it. But since I'm not running anymore, I decide to switch it up a little. One day I spot a flier on the community board. Yoga classes Mondays and Wednesdays at 9:00 am.

~

We're in a seated twist pose. The teacher pads barefoot around the room assisting, adjusting. His voice smooth. Instructions clear. Cues easy to follow.

Plus, he exudes that mysterious something else. While he doesn't talk about God, or yoga philosophy per se, he conveys that what we are doing is not the same as when we're moving through the circuit or taking a step class.

Months later, I discover he's teaching foundations of Ashtanga yoga. His classes swell in numbers. The gym is a business after all, and lucky for me, they add another asana class and meditation.

~

Scottsdale Community College – Basic Math, English, Psychology, Cultural Anthropology 101. Physical Education. Beginning Hatha Yoga.

Math is definitely not my new best friend. We struggle. A lot. But English, Psych and Anthropology are pathways into awareness, insight and discovery. Heaven.

And yoga, well the minute I step foot on the mat, I'm home. Again. Who knew that in a few short years I'd be teaching, semester after semester, right in that same room at Scottsdale Community College?

~

The yoga is good. Instructors skilled. Yet, something is off for me. I'm not sure what.

Second Marriage: check.

Motherhood: a big, fat zero.

~

We're riding our bikes along the golf course. 5:00 am. The sun slowly emerging from the inky night. Bold strokes of reddish gold. Orange. Pinky-purple. Camelback Mountain a silhouette in the distance. We stop. Bikes side by side. Steve reaches over and clasps my hand. Smiles. My heart softens when I spot his crooked front tooth.

Smile gone. Pensive. "Why don't we adopt?"

"What?"

"Why don't we adopt?"

"I thought that's what you said. How long have you been thinking about this?"

"What difference does it make?"

"I don't know. Just seems like it's coming out of nowhere."

"Baby. We gotta get our lives back. You're whacked out most of the time with all the crap you're on. I can't keep doing this. Neither can you. It's like we're sealed inside a pressure cooker and one of us is going to blow."

I shiver in the early-morning light, though it's already eighty-five degrees.

"We want a family. Right?"

"But he or she won't have your crooked smile. Your curly hair."

"Does that really matter?"

~

I miss my mother. I long to sit at her kitchen table. Sip coffee. Nibble her freshly baked biscotti. Lay my head in her lap and hand over my burdens. I don't bother picking up the phone. Instead, I make a list of all the grocery items needed and head to the store.

Searching the pantry, I pull down the old, dented stainless-steel pot. Swipe the inside clean with a damp paper towel and place it on the stove. Pour extra-virgin imported Italian olive oil in the center and turn the gas to medium-high. Next, I mince two cloves of garlic and chop a small, white onion. Gliding my knife along the cutting board, I slide them into sizzling golden oil.

Waiting till the onions turn translucent and the garlic slightly brown, I open one large can of peeled tomatoes. One large can of tomato puree. And splash both into the pot. The kitchen explodes with the sweet, pungent flavor of home.

Chapter Nine
~~I Am Waiting~~

I'm terrified I won't be a good mother. Steve and I are sitting in a circle with seven other couples in a cold, damp room on the first floor of St. Luke's Hospital. The twenty-three-year-old young woman leading the program is an adult adoptee. She presses her finger down on an ancient cassette tape recorder. The room fills with the howling of an infant. She releases her finger on the button and proceeds to do this a total of four times.

Four different wails. We, the prospective adoptive parents, are supposed to recognize and write down what kind of cry it is. *I'm hungry. I'm wet. I want to be held. My belly aches.* Steve scores perfectly.

It's dark and raining. We run to the car. I slam the door shut and start sobbing.

"Maybe I'm not supposed to be a mother. I couldn't tell one cry from the other. It's all just wailing to me."

He turns, pulling me into his arms. "It's okay. You're just scared."

~

We're referred to an adoption attorney in Los Angeles. One month later we hop a plane to meet him. He's a pioneer in this field, representing biological and adoptive parents for twenty-five years and specializing in open or semi-open adoptions. At six foot two he's Cary Grant handsome, with a wide smile, firm handshake and kind eyes.

While he takes his time, and gives us breaks, the interview process is six grueling hours long. At the end, he tells us that it will take about eight months to one year to find a match. His methodology is principled, ethical, diligent and compassionate to all parties.

Three weeks later, his office calls. "Can you fly in on Friday? We think we've found a match."

~

Adoptive and biological parents are not to meet until formally introduced by the attorney. The office is set up with separate entrances. We ride up on the elevator with a very pregnant teenage girl/woman and an older woman about Steve's age. Neither one turns to look at us. All four of us walk off on the same floor, entering the attorney's office through the appropriately designated doors.

Steve and I look at one another. Simultaneously, "You think that was her?"

Two hours later, Steve and I are still waiting to be called into the attorney's inner sanctum. My hands are slick with sweat, and I wipe them on a disintegrating tissue. I focus on my breath. Breathe in. Breathe out. The receptionist asks if we'd like coffee. I whisper no thank you. My bladder is already on high alert.

When the receptionist finally calls out our names, I jump. Seated around the small conference table sit the two women from the elevator. This time, the very pregnant young woman levels her unwavering blue eyes directly into mine. Black dots swirl in front of me. My throat constricts and no words form. Breathe in. Breathe out.

She smiles, revealing perfect little white teeth. Steve speaks first, giving me a moment to pull it together.

Like a master orchestra conductor, the attorney leads us through deep, deliberate, exploratory questions.

At the end of five hours, my mouth is a desert. I'm sweating through my silk blouse, my hands once again slimy.

I ask to be excused, and jerk my way to the ladies' room. Looking in the mirror, I stare back at a pasty gray impression of myself. I wash my hands. Dip a paper towel under the faucet and wipe my face, neck and under my arms.

Before I open the door to the office, I hear the sound of laughter. Despite my raging anxiety, my skin softens.

The young woman reaches across her chair and hands me an ultrasound photograph of her unborn baby boy.

"You can't keep it. I just want you to be able to see him."

Holding back an onslaught of tears I manage, "Okay."

With a wisdom and clarity that astounds, she looks at Steve first, smiles, then holds me spellbound. "I'm really glad you're together. It's nice. But even if you were alone, I'd want you to be his mother."

For several seconds, both our fingers remain wrapped around the edges of the photo. I will my fingers to release their grip.

Chapter Ten
~~*Language of The Soul*~~

We pause in the courtyard of the concert hall, waiting for my mother and father to arrive. It's ninety-three degrees at 6:30 pm, with a slight breeze blowing through the palm fronds.

Steve's wearing a Hawaiian shirt. Light-blue background, "Aloha" printed in black letters and hula dancers waving their arms. Khaki slacks, deck shoes, no socks. I'm dressed in a flowing, honey-colored linen skirt. Flip flops, black sleeveless top, with a cardigan sweater thrown over my shoulders.

The intimate auditorium holds 500 people. We find our seats about halfway down the rows in the center of the aisle. The stage is elevated.

My skin tingles. Seated between Steve and my mother, I hold each of their hands.

Commencement begins. The gangling, giggling teens walk, strut, or plow across the stage to receive their high school diplomas.

The principal congratulates each one, and they saunter away.

I reach down into my purse for a tissue. When I look up again, a young man is already moving towards the end of the stage to exit. He stops. Then, turning, he searches the crowd until he meets our eyes. Moving from me to Steve and back again.

Even from a distance, his eyes are a startling crystal blue. Cheeks round, still with the flesh of unshed youth. His smile conspiratorial as he tips his graduation cap in our direction.

Blood pounds in my ears, drowning out any other sound. I squeeze Steve's and my mother's hands. Tears fill my eyes.

"It's him," I choke out.

"Of course it's him," Steve whispers.

"No. Him."

~

I surface slowly, not wanting to break through the waters. Turning, I cocoon into the back side of my husband's warmth, and wrap my arm around his waist. In his sleep, he reaches back and pulls me tighter.

My lips pressing against his back, I breathe, "Steve, he found us."

~

I'm still floating in the currents of the dream when I hear jabbering through the baby monitor. 4:00 am. Easing quietly away from my slumbering husband, I tumble out of bed. Pulling on my robe, I slide my feet into slippers and walk down the hall to our son's room. I stop. Listen. Peek in. The soft nightlight fills the room with shadows. He's sitting up in his crib. Unafraid. Immersed in conversation with his favorite stuffed animal, christened Roger Rabbit.

"Morning, Buddy; you're up early."

He stands. Sticks Roger's ear in his mouth, reaches out and wraps chubby arms around my neck. I breathe deep, inhaling the mysterious, sweet, maple scent of him. Changing his diaper, I lean down and trail kisses across his tummy. He laughs out loud, mending the cracks in my heart.

In the dark of early morning, his blue eyes shine brilliant. The tiniest star speckle of brown glitters in his left iris. Swaddling him in a light flannel blanket, I hold him close, rocking to and fro. An old jazz classic that my dad and aunt used to sing, suddenly a lullaby.

"When you're smiling, when you're smiling, the whole world smiles with you. When you're laughing, when you're laughing, the whole world laughs with you. But when you're crying, you bring on the rain, so stop your sighing, be happy again, 'cause when you're smiling, when you're smiling, the whole world smiles with you."

~

It's Mother's Day. Steve and our son carry a breakfast tray into the bedroom and place it on my lap. Warm orange juice. A cold egg, no longer over easy, and burnt toast. The most delicious meal I've ever tasted. We plan a drive down to Half Moon Bay for a picnic lunch on the beach.

We're just about packed and ready to go when out bursts, "I'm mad at you, Mommy."

"Why?"

"Because."

"Well, that's not really a reason. Did I hurt your feelings? What did I do to make you mad?"

I sit down on the floor. "It's okay. You can tell me."

Tears, and a push with his little fists on my shoulders.

"What's going on, Bud?"

"I'm mad 'cause I didn't grow in your tummy."

My eyes fill. I thought I was ready for this. I read the books. Took adoptive parenting classes. Talked to friends. Yet, nothing, nothing prepared me for having my heart eviscerated.

I open my arms, but he stands there. Planted like a sturdy little tree.

He's not done. "Michael grew in his mommy's tummy."

"I know, Buddy. I wish you grew in my tummy too. But you know where you did grow?"

He jerks his head no.

Reaching for his closed fist I gently open his fingers and place his toddler hand on the center of my chest. "Here. You grew here, in my heart."

Taking hold of his other hand, I hold it and breathe. Then, I place our joined hands on his little chest.

"Every time you get mad, or sad, just put your hand on your heart and remember how much Mommy loves you."

Breathe in. Breathe out. "Should we get your baby book and look at all the photos? I can tell you your story again, of when you were born."

Seconds... eternal.

His blonde curls sway. Turning, he points to the front door and in a decent imitation of his dad, bellows, "To the beach!"

Chapter Eleven
~~*Melancholia*~~

My dad was only seven years old when his mother died. He was the youngest of four. Two older brothers, a sister, then him. A year ago, I asked my then eighty-nine-year-old dad what he remembered about his mother, my paternal grandmother.

He put his head down. Several moments later he lifted his teary eyes, looked into mine and choked, "I don't have any memories. Except I remember hearing that she died of a broken heart."

Growing up, we weren't very close to my dad's side of the family. On the occasional Thanksgiving or Christmas when we did visit his stepmother, his siblings and my cousins, I felt apprehensive.

Entering the house, I felt the air tremble with the vestige of scandal. I'd cling to my mother or brothers like a life preserver. My aunts and uncles treated us with kindness. There was conversation. Laughter. But the moment we all climbed back into the car, I'd sense a collective sigh of relief.

It wasn't until I was a teenager that I learned the truth. Or kernels of it. My paternal grandfather left my grandmother for a married woman, who happened to have three children of her own. And if that wasn't disruptive enough, the other woman just happened to be his sister-in-law. Not long after my grandfather remarried, his first wife, my paternal grandmother, died suddenly. This was definitely a classic cluster fuck.

The older kids moved out on their own. But my dad, my seven-year-old dad, was sent to live with his father, whom he barely knew, and his stepmother. She stood about five-foot tall and was almost as wide, with a voice that barked and snarled. Just to be clear, the first cousins he'd grown up with were now legally his siblings. Yep, a shit-pile.

A few years ago, I was collecting photos to create a family montage for a central wall in my home. Realizing that I didn't have any of my dad's mother and father, I asked my folks.

I picked up the old sepia photo of my grandmother, and saw a young woman, probably in her late thirties. Her light-brown hair was pinned back, head slightly bowed, and her deep, dark eyes stared off into the distance.

I've always been told that I bear a strong resemblance to my maternal grandmother. So, I was totally taken off guard.

With unsteady hands and voice, "Oh my gosh. Dad. I look like your mother."

Her sadness touched deep inside, where the wellspring of melancholia that I've wrestled with since childhood, and fought to understand, lived on in me. I carried it. I was the guardian of my grandmother's despair.

Later that night, I stood in front of the mirror, holding my grandmother's photo up alongside my face, and sure enough, there she was.

I probed a little deeper, and learned that it was rumored that my dad's mother took her own life. But there's no proof. Families not only safeguard secrets; they also gossip. While she hadn't been sick, the evidence showed that her grief and the burden of raising four children as an uneducated immigrant took their toll.

"Dad, are you sure you don't remember anything about your mother? Not one thing?"

"She had a beautiful smile."

~

At seventeen, my maternal grandmother and her older sister Teresa sailed from the port of Bari, Italy to Ellis Island. Their brother Frank sponsored them and helped to arrange marriage for my grandmother, Philomena, to his friend Tom, my grandfather. The two young women traveled by train from New York City to Chicago. They spoke no English.

My grandmother had been in love with a soldier who died in World War I. And while my grandfather wasn't a stranger to her, they weren't friends. Not lovers. Unreal as it seems to me, it was only two generations preceding my own that a woman in my family was married by arrangement.

The interesting and beautiful thing is that it was a good marriage. Created and bonded by mutual necessity, it developed into love. They had five children together: Daniel, Isabel, Rocco, Anthony and my mother, Maddalena.

You've heard about Rocky, my gambling charismatic uncle. What I haven't told you is that he was in the infantry during World War II, a medic who worked hard to save lives. He never wanted to speak about what he saw. How he bore witness to so much blood, sorrow and death. Learning this about him when I got older explained a lot to me.

~

And, the rest of the clan.

Tony was the family's golden boy. Sweet. Handsome. Kind. And rock solid. He made his mother laugh and swear in Italian by untying her apron strings while she was cooking, canning or baking. His sisters adored him. His brothers found camaraderie and kinship.

Instead of enlisting in the Army, like his older brother Rocky, Tony proudly joined the Navy and was assigned to a freighter. It was two years after the United States entered the war, in 1943, when off the coast of Florida two American ships collided, resulting in a mass inferno. Details of the horrific event remain unclear today as officers and navigators from both vessels did not survive. Like many who were lost, Tony's body was never recovered.

Initially, there was speculation as to whether the freighters had been torpedoed by a German submarine. The truth too may be buried with the victims. Consensus: As it was a required blackout night the ships' radar simply did not detect one other.

My grandmother was fifty-years old when he died. My mom tells me that her mother, Philomena, never ate fish again, since her son's burial ground was the unfathomable depth of the ocean.

Isabel was always more delicate than her little sister, my mother. Ten years older, she had one foot more rooted in the old ways of Southern Italy – while my mother struggled to be "American." In speech, dress, food and friends.

When Tony was killed, something in my aunt died with him. She turned inward. Eventually, she married a man who was near the age of her father. It was stabilizing for her. They had two children, who soon became honorary Nordica Kids. We sensed, even though we were young, that Auntie Isabel's heart was sad. Fragile.

Yet when she smiled, a veil lifted, and we caught a glimpse of the free young woman she once had been. My aunt loved us kids the same as Dolly did. Just more quietly. More restrained. Held in. Almost as if she knew that if she let her love pour out, somehow, she'd melt away.

To make my Christmas Eve birthday special, she'd bake me a cake shaped liked an evergreen tree. While my mom was the cook, Isabel was the baker. I can still taste the green-tinted cream cheese frosting and the moist bite of warm carrot cake.

And then there was Danny. He's a hard one. I didn't know him like Rocky and Isabel. He was often estranged from the family. My uncle carried the legacy of alcoholism. He fought his demons for as long as I can remember.

Yet, there was a sweet gentleness about him when he wasn't drinking. Handsome in a completely different way from his brothers. His cheeks were round and pink, most likely from the alcohol. But back then he appeared jolly, his nose straight and full. He didn't wear the look of a Southern Italian.

One holiday (it must have been Thanksgiving or Christmas, because the temps were frigid), I heard a knock on the kitchen door. And there he stood. Tall. Imposing. Wearing a dark blue-and-green plaid coat with a gray suede fedora covering his head. A wool scarf wrapped around his neck, but no gloves.

An unmoving mountain. I'm not sure if he saw me or not. Face red and chapped. Tears stinging his eyes. I look around the kitchen for reinforcements. No one.

I reach out and take his big, cold hand in mine. "Uncle Danny, come on in. It's cold outside."

When he died, my mother cried for days. I'd hear her praying. Relieved his suffering was finally over. Grieved that his life was riddled with contradiction.

~

The real estate market in Arizona, and all over the country, takes a major downturn. My husband is offered a job in the San Francisco Bay Area. We've been hit hard financially and our choices are limited. So, we go.

I don't know a soul in San Francisco except Steve and our three-year-old. Some days it feels as if I've been placed in the witness protection program. Hiding in plain sight.

I'm a mess. Ruminating on the thought that I'm a horrible mother. Crazy wife. Like a pipe near bursting, both my head and my insides were ready to explode. For the first six months that we live in San Mateo, I plan our outings around the location of the nearest bathroom.

One night we're sitting in the little den, reading. I circle a mention in the neighborhood paper advertising a mother's club. Though not affiliated with any religion, the monthly meetings are held at a nearby church. Weekly playdates are arranged, according to the age of your children.

The women who make up this group hold master's degrees as if they were menus. They've run Fortune 500 companies, catering businesses, and restaurants. Their art is shown in galleries and their published books named "Pick of the Week." They litigate and instigate. Investigate and report. They design clothing and earthquake-resistant buildings, and run the evening like it's a formal corporate board meeting.

Siting in the circle, I barely squeak out my name before I run for the bathroom. Then sneak out the side door. I don't return.

Three months later, the founder of the organization calls. Invites me for coffee. Though she's two years younger than I am, I feel like a child in her presence.

Slowly she lights me up with her enthusiasm, her insight into parenting, her dedication, and her hand of friendship. Before I know it, I'm in. Two feet in. Heart in. On committees in. Saving my sanity and my child's life, and possibly my marriage in.

A handful of these accomplished women confide in me that they feel isolated. Sad. Not soul-fed. I listen and think, "Are you kidding me?" They live in gracious homes. Have developed great support systems. Enjoy financial success, handsome husbands and beautiful children. I wonder, "What the hell?" Yet, I'm curious. Drawn.

So, this little band from the mother's club forms a spirituality group. We alternate leading and offering content we believe to be inspiring and informative. Pertinent and exploratory. Evocative and provocative.

There's a corner in my mind that never feels that I quite belong. I'm an imposter. When it's my turn to lead, no matter how prepared or turned on I am by my topic (usually mysticism or meditation), I shrink.

~

"Sorry, my mommy can't talk to you." I hear my son's voice as his bare feet patter on the saltillo tile in the kitchen. Answering a phone that's too big for his hand.

"She's in time out. No, she wasn't bad. She's med-e-ating." Boom. He clicks off.

I feel the rush of him as he enters the bedroom. Sitting across from me, he touches my knee and whispers, "Me too, Mommy."

I open my eyes just as he closes his. He sits for about, hmm, maybe thirty seconds. Then jumps up. Kisses my cheek and runs off again.

~

Shrinking or not, there's one woman who can't be denied. She's a quiet force of nature. Five foot eleven, with thick, shoulder-length hair. You can't just call it red. That'd be too ordinary. The sun catches streaks of cinnamon, gold and russet that set her fine features aglow. Her lilting accent is hard to determine, as she speaks several languages fluently.

We meet at the park with our four-year-old boys and their instantaneous friendship fuels our connection. For three years, we support one another with the raising of our boys and the daily challenges of life.

One day, we're talking about desires and tarnished dreams.

"Dear," her sweet parlance for those she cares about, "Why not go back to college?"

~

These new sisters of mine stir the fire of long-buried aspirations. I register for a Cultural Anthropology class at the College of San Mateo. The instructor is a progressive New Jersey transplant who hasn't lost his East Coast accent. He's a caricature. Tall, lanky, he strides around the front of the room in quick, sharp movements. His thick, graying, wild hair needs a haircut and shampoo. White flecks dust the shoulders of his untucked shirt. He captivates and ignites my imagination. The classroom is filled to capacity. Who knew?

At the end of the semester, he asks us to pick up our grades in his office. I wait my turn while talking with one of my classmates. Many of them are taking his class for the second time, simply because.

~

It's three years since we've moved to San Francisco, and Steve is offered an opportunity to return to Phoenix. I beg him to let us stay. No chance. Less than two months later, we're unpacking boxes, smack dab back in the heart of Snottsdale.

"I'm not exactly sure what I mean by this, but I just have to say it."

"Okay, go for it."

"I don't want to go back to the life we lived before."

"I'm not exactly sure what you mean either, but we'll figure it out."

And in just the way my son holds securely onto his trusted best friend Roger Rabbit, I hold onto to a burgeoning new me.

~

I walk into his office and he asks me to sit down. Handing me a printout of my grade, he says, "I noticed you didn't register for any classes next semester. Can I ask you why?"

"We're moving back to Arizona."

"Well, I hope that's what you want."

For a charismatic teacher, he's not a great communicator. Stumbling over his words, finally, "You're a good writer. Insightful. I hope you keep at it. Don't let your mind and talent go to waste."

~

From Target, we've picked out pencils and a pack of colored Post-it Notes shaped like hearts. My son is learning to print, and we're sitting up at the kitchen counter. Once a week we choose a word. A virtue.

"Okay, Bud, what does kindness mean?"

"Mmm... like when you're playing with a friend, and they fall down and you help them up?"

"Yeah, that's kindness. So, which color sticky note does kindness look like to you?"

"Blue."

"Great. I'll print it first, then you get to copy and print it on your blue heart paper. Now, let's stick one on the fridge and you choose where to put the other one."

While we work and play together on this project, I think back to my old hippy professor. I choose a pink Post-it Note, and in big block letters spell out *Imagination*.

Chapter Twelve
~~*The Year of Ten*~~

Sitting back into the softness of the cushion, I'm immediately enveloped by the wings of my reading chair and the familiar comfort of routine. I close my eyes as thoughts begin swirling around the edges of my mind like whirling dervishes dancing in trance. I shift excitedly, and instantly the dance of thoughts disappears. Okay, I tell myself, so that's how inspiration comes. Elusive. Mysterious, like mist rising from a marsh. I take a few breaths and wait. I breathe in and ask for patience.

Again, memory and inspiration begin to play a game of hide-and-seek while I breathe in, breathe out. I sense a memory taking a tentative step forward. Be patient, I caution, as I carefully unveil the precious, fragile gift. The mists part and the boon enlivens. Vividly, I see my son as a skinny, ten-year-old boy, standing proud and defiant on a soccer field. He's wearing long, white tube socks that reach just under his knobby knees, which are crossed with Ninja Turtle Band-Aids, marking him like a badge of honor. The parting of the mist continues, revealing a treasure chest of memories as one by one they come spilling forth. Each memory like a precious stone, multi-faceted and rich with emotion, these gems take shape and form. Breathing in and out, I focus on one particular shimmering jewel.

~

He crawls underneath the covers, props himself up with his well-loved pillow and cries, "Come on, Mom, it's your turn to read. Prince Caspian is in trouble!"

I climb onto the bed beside him and snuggle myself close. Kissing his freshly scrubbed cheek, I take in the smell of his bubblegum toothpaste and marvel that he is my child. Ringlets, the color of golden wheat, frame eyes that flash green as an angry cat when frightened or cranky, and deep blue when happy. Cautiously I check: blue or green? Yes, this will be a smooth read.

~

On my son's tenth birthday, we began reading *The Chronicles of Narnia.* We read together nightly, alternating one paragraph for him, one page for me. Almost to the day, one year later, we completed the set of seven books and knighted our shared experience "The Year of Ten." Some may say the rekindled bond of mother and son happened by chance, while others may say such a result pure fortune. What do you say?

At that time in our lives, I found myself examining my own son much the way a research scientist examines a new strain of bacteria. "Oh my, what do we have developing here? This can't possibly be my son." I never imagined a child of mine to be so frightfully a "boy-child." He was much like the rough-and-ready brand of jeans he wore. Tough and eager for a challenge as he pulled further and further away from me. Gone were the days of sitting on the floor playing with tumbling blocks and Uno, laughing and being silly. Now, on my suggestion, his response was often, "No way – that's girl stuff," or, "Mom, can Michael come over? He's more fun."

Realization dawns that the lazy hours spent sweetly together are lost to younger years. Not understanding this new – and not-improved – relationship with my son, I felt sadness seep into my bones. Days before the big tenth birthday, I wandered aimlessly down aisle after aisle of the toy store, praying for the perfect gift for a little person I no longer knew. Heading to the gaming section, I was mystified by the allure of violent Game Boy and Nintendo games. Totally frustrated, I left. For several moments, my feet stuck to the cement, preventing me from moving.

Finally, in desperation, I entered a neighboring bookstore. Just standing inside the hallowed walls, my heart began to tap dance. A young man wearing a rumpled shirt, a tie yanked to the left and with his beard in sad need of a trim lurched towards me.

"Can I help you, Ma'am?"

"Yes, I'm looking for a book for my son's tenth birthday. He's learning to read chapter books, and he's finding it difficult and frustrating."

"Well he might be a little young yet, but *The Chronicles of Narnia* were some of my favorites. They still are."

Having never read them myself, I sit down and peruse the books. Will he like them? Is this something we can read together? The longer I sit, the more I feel calm washing over me – and a plan begins to formulate. I compromise. I'll buy him a Nintendo game and we will read *The Chronicles* together.

The day of the big birthday bash arrives, and after the games are played, well-wishes are given and the cake is devoured, it's time to open the long-awaited gifts. I watch as my son grows more and more excited with each present torn into. Now I'm no longer sure of the decision I've made. I know he'll hate it.

Finally, after attacking all the gifts except his dad's and mine, he grabs the two solitary packages and rips into them. The Nintendo game is the first opened, and he jumps up and down, crying in a frenzy, "Yes! Yes!"

My heart thumps against my chest as he tears into the last gift. "What? Mom, books." He tosses them aside without a backward glance, and like a pack of wild dogs, the boys rush to sit in front of the television, frothing at the mouth, waiting for the Nintendo game to begin.

Not to be undone, later that evening after our nighttime ritual was nearly complete, I sit on his bed with the first book, *The Magician's Nephew*, held firmly in my hand.

"Okay, Young Man, now it's my turn. Do you want to read first, or should I?"

"This is stupid. I don't want to read. I hate reading."

"All right then. I'll begin. Chapter One. *The Wrong Door*. This is the story about something that happened long ago..."

And so began our mutual discovery and journey through the magic and lure of *The Chronicles of Narnia*, by C.S. Lewis.

~

Hearing the chimes of my cell phone ringing, I'm pulled back into the moment, where I sit in the quiet of my home.

"Hello?"

"Hi, Mom. What are you doing?"

"Believe it or not, I was just sitting here, thinking about you."

"Oh yeah – what're you thinking?"

"I was wondering. What's one of your favorite childhood memories?"

With hardly a pause, I listen to the deep resonance of my son's voice, "Mom, do you really have to ask? It's The Year of Ten."

Chapter Thirteen
~ *Unfinished Business*~

The worn, tattered biscotti recipe in my mother's handwriting is clipped to the stand so that both she and I can read it. All of the baking ingredients are measured out before we begin. Just the way my mother likes it. Just as her mother did.

Today it's my turn to bake the well-loved Italian biscuit while my mother supervises, adding her wise tips along the way. It's a simple cookie recipe, but not an easy one to make. My grandmother's biscotti were the best in the family. Once a week she visited relatives. Many were ill and not able to leave their homes. My grandmother never failed to arrive without a plastic tub, carefully and lovingly packed. It was expected, and much appreciated, by the recipient. Now my mother's cookies have taken her place in the lineage of biscotti baking. My aunt, my mother's sister, is a prima baker herself.

They think we adult kids don't know it, but secretly my aunt and my mother are competing to rank as Numero Uno. Let's just say – regardless of who made the biscuit you bite into, you're blasted with the flavor of anise or almond. Baked correctly, they are light, with just the perfect amount of crunch. They taste nothing like the pre-packaged, hard-to-bite, hard-to-swallow, tasteless store-bought versions. Genuine biscotti, made from an authentic recipe, are true nirvana. One day, maybe, I might come in a decent third or fourth.

The dough is sticky to the touch. And the handling of it must be done with love and patience. The love, I'm overflowing with, but the patience... well, that's another matter. It was one of the virtues I chose to print on my own Post-it Notes.

I've dropped my son off at kindergarten, so I have the morning to enjoy with my mother. When we brought our son home, only days old, my mother was on a plane from Chicago to Phoenix before I picked up diapers from the grocery. Within a month, my folks sold their hair salon business, their beloved home, and moved to Arizona to be near us.

My dad was the only one who was able to get our baby to take a nap. He walked him, all the while crooning him to sleep. The song that seemed to be magic was *Smoke Gets in Your Eyes*. I admit our lullaby selection was a bit unusual.

The project was a success, and now my mother and I are enjoying our freshly baked and still-warm cookies. We have two each. One we eat plain, and the other, we dip each bite into our steaming mugs of hot coffee. If you haven't tried it – trust me, you will never be the same.

Our conversation darts from one topic to another, mimicking the hummingbird we watch outside her window.

"So, are you ready to tell me what's really going on with you?"

I look into her eyes, trying to avoid the truth, but with my mother there's no subterfuge.

"You know the other night when you babysat... so I could meet Steve after work with some of his coworkers?"

She gives me a couple of minutes. Finally, "Go on."

"Well, there's this new woman who works there. She's a few years younger than me. Pretty... long, brown hair... long legs... athletic..."

Then, like a missile, it comes shooting out of my mouth, "And big frickin' boobs that she practically shoved into Steve's face. Jesus. I couldn't believe it. She couldn't care less that I was there. She was practically all over him."

"And...?"

"And the bitch of it was that he liked it."

"Well I hate to say it, but most men would."

"But I didn't think he was most men. I thought he was different."

"Were you drinking?"

"I wasn't, but everyone else was. You know, I could see him looking at me. Like he knew he was just barely this side of the line."

"And...?"

"I finally stood up, grabbed my purse, casually announced I was leaving and started to walk away. He left too, and when we got home I went ballistic."

"Did you feel better?"

"Not really."

"Well, talk to him when you've calmed down. And explain how it made you feel. Ask him how he'd feel if it were reversed."

"You know, Mom, it pisses me off. What is it with guys?"

"I hate to say it, but most men's brains reside in their penis."

~

Bam. I realized that the whole of my attention had shifted, and was now placed on our son. That I was slowly but steadily forgetting what it meant to be "in love." Sure, I was a loving wife. But my world was shrinking. Narrowing down to motherhood. My sole focus now was raising a child.

No longer did I yearn for more, outside of the circle of the nuclear family we created. My son was now everything to me. And in that smack of recognition, I began to lose the anger that I felt building up inside of me like an old coal furnace.

It was *me* who was going through the motions – wife, friend and lover. It was *me* who was allowing my relationship with my husband to slip through my fingers. Plus, what the hell was I doing? Placing the whole of me onto my little boy was unfair to him as well. It was stifling, over-protective and damn unhealthy.

So, I did what would become a lifelong "go to" for me. As a retired barber and daughter of hairstylists, I had my hair chopped off. Then, every day, I looked in the mirror and spoke out loud, "Oh yeah, I remember you – you sassy little thing. Time to take the high road, Baby."

After my conversation with my mother, something started to nag at me. Itch. I invited it to come to the surface. In time, it did. So, at the very next opportunity, I asked her something like this.

"Mom, remember years ago... on your birthday?" I don't need to say which birthday. She knows exactly what I was referring to.

My mother, standing at the kitchen sink, turns to look over her shoulder at me.

"You want to know if your dad really did have an affair." It was more of a statement than a question. "I'm surprised it took you this long to ask me."

"Well, Mom, honestly, I forced myself to forget about that night. Just stashed it away like it never happened. But that doesn't really work, does it?"

"No, it doesn't. And since we're being honest here, I really don't know what happened that night. Your dad denied they had an affair. But did something go on?"

"I never liked her. When I was a kid, helping out at the salon, I'd watch her. With Dad. You. Her clients. I don't know – she seemed manipulative. As if she had an agenda, beyond the job she was hired to do."

"She and her husband were having problems. When she apologized to me, after the dinner fiasco, she confessed to using Dad to make her husband jealous. She felt ignored and unseen by him." My mother makes a quote motion in the air.

"I can believe that. That guy was in a world of his own. Or should I say a Budweiser world? Still, that was a really nasty thing for her to do. Why do women tear each other apart like that? Deliberately hurting someone is bullshit. It could have destroyed your marriage."

My mother continued to wash the dishes. The silence felt heavy, until she sliced through it with, "In my generation, we didn't have many female role models. It's different today. I'm happy for you that you're part of a new paradigm, and a champion for other women."

"So, how did you get over it?"

"Hmm... I had four kids depending on me, so it wasn't like I could just walk away. It took a lot out of me, but eventually I decided to stop dwelling on it and move forward. Plus, your dad was so sorry. Contrite. Which actually didn't help my suspicions any, since he's not one to apologize. But I drew a line in the sand of my mind – and started over."

~

My advisor calls me into her office.

"Except for Math and Algebra, you're getting all A's. Those two subjects pulled your grade point average down a bit, but you're acing all the honors classes. I'd like you to consider applying to the university. ASU has some great programs."

I shake my head no.

"Why?"

"The campus is huge. Overwhelming. Can't do it."

"Do some research. Check out other options. Phoenix College. Or better yet, Prescott College has a great ADP – Adult Degree Program. It might be a perfect fit for you."

It is. My new advisor, also perfect. She's in charge of making sure I keep the degree credible. Not too "woo-woo," she calls it.

"Sure, Paulette. You can take Reiki classes and become a Reiki master. However, it absolutely will not count as credit towards your Transpersonal Psychology degree."

But a Depth Psychology class, taught by a Jungian psychologist, where we study dreams as a therapy modality, sure does. Part of my homework. Keeping a personal dream journal.

~

College degree: Prescott College, B.A., Transpersonal Psychology – check.

Yoga certifications: Integrative Yoga Therapy, E-RYT 500, Anusara® School of Hatha Yoga – check.

~

My son is maybe eleven years old. It's teacher development day at school, so we're home together. I'm cranky as hell. I don't know why. It's just this scratchy, squiggly feeling that starts on the inside and works its way to my skin. I try baking. Put Van the Man on loud. Nothing.

"Mom, isn't it your practice day?"

Since he was a little boy, I've been attending a "teacher practice" class with a group of friends. We meet Tuesdays and Thursdays for three hours, and work our way through the Anusara asana syllabus. It's a tough, kick-ass kind of class. We're there for the connection, and to help each other learn and advance our asana practice. Each class begins with a ten-minute chant called the *Hanuman Chalisa*. The chant is a tribute to the Monkey God, who offers his life in service to his friends, the God Ram and the Goddess Sita. Everything Hanuman does, he does in deference to God, whom Ram and Sita represent.

We western yogis chant this song in Sanskrit as a way to honor the practice, and one another, as we work towards embodying the qualities of love and service. Most of my friends have beautiful, strong voices, and they belt out as we sing along with Krishna Das on his CD. Me, I love it, but I squeak out the Sanskrit words. Listen a lot.

As asana practitioners, we view our bodies as vehicles, in which we aspire to be like the archetype of the Monkey God. Hanuman is also funny, smart and loyal. Who doesn't want more of that?

But today I choose not to go, and leave my son home alone for several hours. It's the age of World of Warcraft. The online computer game that connects with players around the planet. I have no doubt that the moment I walk out the door for the hour drive there, three hours of practice and another hour ride home, my son will be sitting in front of the computer screen, eating potato chips he's stashed in his closet and downing Dr. Pepper.

When emotions get too pent-up, I work through it all on my mat. After all these years of practice, I've trained my body to respond as a release valve. No need for talk therapy at this point. Just throw down the mat and practice.

"Yeah, you're right. I'll go practice outside for a little while. When I'm through, we'll fix lunch."

It amazes me that this kid is so in tune with the rhythms around him. He chose not to speak until he was three. Other than "Momma" and "Dada," not much else. But you could see that nothing was getting by him. Then one day, riding in the car, he starts to speak in full sentences. These days, though, as a pre-teen, he's gone back to the more silent times. I need to pay attention for the signals he sends. Through the changing color and depth of emotion in his eyes. The way he holds his body. The tilt of his head. All speak to me louder than any words.

But the thing is – I need to pay attention, or I'll miss the silent signals he's sending. That's the yoga. Because of him, I want to be better.

"Good idea, Mom."

~

The house is quiet. My Steves are off to work and school. Cleaning up the kitchen after the rush of breakfast, I'm surprised by the ring of the phone. I hesitate answering, but the caller ID shows it's my best friend from Chicago.

"Hey, Paul."

We've know each other since we were in the third and fourth grade. Immediately, my radar is up.

"What's wrong?"

"Nothing. Really."

"Kath... what's going on?"

"He called me and wants to know if you'll talk to him." She need not say his name. I know.

"Are you kidding me? What for?"

"I don't know. He just said it was important. And that you probably wouldn't want me to give him your unlisted number, so he gave me his. He asked if you'd call him. I told him I didn't know if you would, or if I'd even get hold of you right away."

"What the fuck. You think he's okay? Sick?"

"I don't know, Paul. I'm as surprised as you."

"Jesus, I don't know if I can do this."

~

Try as I might, I can't remember our last real goodbye. The last time I saw his face. Did we hug? Cry? Hold on to one another, afraid to let go? Or did we pivot and walk away without a backward glance? But damn, hard as I try, I only remember the last time I heard his voice.

~

I slug down a glass of water. Pick up the phone. Punch in the numbers.

"Hello?"

My response is fighting to be released.

"Hello. Paul. Is that you?"

I want to slam the phone down. Scream. I inhale.

Exhaling, "Yeah, it's me."

Blackout.

"So, how're you doing?"

"I'm doing good. You?"

What I'm doing is my best not to give him an inch. Waiting. Blackout again. Until I can't stand in the silence another minute.

"Are you sick? Is something wrong? Is that why you want to talk to me?"

"Paul, I just want to apologize for hurting you. For everything I did that caused you pain. For messing up our lives."

"Okay."

"Do you accept my apology?"

"Yeah, I do. But you apologized before, so why again? Years later? Why now?"

"When we first split up, even after the divorce was final, we always told each other that one day we'd find our way back. Do you still think one day we'll end up together?"

"Jesus. You're married. I'm married, for Christ's sake. I have a son. Why are you doing this? Oh, I get it, you finally left your wife, didn't you?"

"Okay, forget it; let's leave it at I'm truly sorry for hurting you."

"Let me ask you something now. Are you in some kind of twelve-step program? Making amends?"

"Why; would that make a difference for you? Would that give me a chance?"

"No, it doesn't make a difference. Except to say if you are, I'm happy for you. I hope it helps you find your way back to yourself."

Dead air, but for the sound of our breathing.

"Paul..."

"Look, you apologized. If you need to hear the words again, yes, I forgive you. You know that a part of me will always love you. Nothing will take that away. But I have to hang up now. This is my life, and I love my husband."

~

Ever since Ms. Slater in the third grade, I wanted to be a teacher. To walk into the classroom as she did, wearing winged tortoiseshell glasses. Red suits with white, starched shirts. Black pumps. Well, maybe not that anymore. Fashions change, and I must say I've never been accused of not having a sense of style.

But I took that dream, and carefully buried it in the depths of my being, all those years before, when I made a promise to a twelve-year-old boy that I'd marry him.

When my brothers and I were little, I'd set up the den like a classroom. They of course were the students, and I was the Ms. Slater impersonator. I'd inhale the smell of the crayons and be carried off to heaven.

So, when my boyfriend, soon-to-be husband, told me he was quitting high school, I was shell-shocked. I begged him not to be so foolish. "What about our future?" I threw at him. "We'll be fine. I'll go to barber school like my brother. He's married with four little kids and making good money."

The imaginary classroom in my mind disintegrated as if it were smoke. I broke down and pleaded my case to his parents and his older brother. No one quits high school anymore. Make him stay and graduate, *please.*

Brick solid walls. How can you make someone see what they don't want to see? Or may be incapable of seeing. Praying to the god I still believed in, I beseeched him. Please, God, make him hear me. Don't let him quit school.

"What about me wanting to be a teacher? Going away to school?"

"You can stay here. You don't need to go away to get your degree. You can commute."

"But how will that be? Me determined to be the first one in my family to earn a college degree and you not finishing high school. It just doesn't jibe."

"Paul, it doesn't make any difference."

But somewhere inside of me, I knew it did.

~

When I was a kid, I was so shy that my family teased me because I could not pick up the phone and place our

Friday-night pizza order. Finally, when I was about eighteen, my mother wrote down on a piece of paper what I was to say, picked up the phone, dialed it, shoved it in my ear and commanded, "Order!"

So, imagine my confusion when years later, I was once again drawn to the teaching world. Initially, I wasn't interested in becoming a teacher. My heart was pulled to the teachings of yoga. The asana practice itself and the philosophy. My teachers encouraged me to stay with the study and to go for training.

Yoga was becoming my spiritual compass, so I took the trainings for my own growth and understanding. This world of yoga was taking me out of myself and expanding me in ways I never dreamed of. In the early days, I did everything I could not to be noticed.

In one of my first trainings, the lead teacher asked the group what our greatest fear was while teaching. While I had many, from remembering the name of poses to sequencing a class, it was chanting the invocation at the beginning of class that freaked me out. I refused to do it.

Of course, as one would have it, each of us was asked to do the thing we feared. Without prior warning, on a sunny morning, high up in the mountains of Utah, in our sweet yoga-training center, I was called upon to chant the blessing. Three times in a row, the classical way, in front of sixty of my peers.

Voice shaky, hands trembling, body ice-cold and sweating, I trip over the Sanskrit words – ending to the applause of my friends. And that was that. I practiced in front of my mirror. Chanted it while driving in my car, and taught it to my son. I took the breath in with each syllable and pushed the breath out with the next.

Wedding Day

Baby Love

Steve, Paulette, Batman

Mom, Dad, Dolly and Rocky

Mom, Dad and the grown up Nordica Kids

Me, Mom, Auntie Isabelle, and Florence

Nana & Papa

Grandma, Grandpa and Kids

Dolly and Mike-the Crooners

Dancing Girl

Communion

Number One Brother, me, Baby Doll and Middle Brother

Nordica House

Christmas 2016

Freedom

LAKSHMI
Part Three

"The rustle of leaves
I hear your voice on the wind
Remembering you
The rustle of leaves
I feel your breath on my cheek
Always loving you"

Chapter Fourteen
~~*Svatantra*~~
"Independent; free, absolute freedom"

I'm driving home from teaching my Tuesday-afternoon yoga class when my cell rings.

I pick it up with a casual hello, oblivious that in the next instant our lives will be forever altered.

It's my best friend's husband. Their son, who happens to be my son's best friend since kindergarten, was in a major car wreck on his way to class at the community college. A construction vehicle ran a red light and plowed into the side of his Honda, pushing him into a tree while never even trying to brake.

Making a U-turn, I change directions and head to my girlfriend's home to pick her up and take her to the hospital. Then I call my husband, sob out the few details I know, and ask him to get home early to be there when our son gets home from school.

This boy-child I love like a son suffers a severe brain injury, never coming out of a coma. Five days later, our friends make the horrific decision to turn off life support. And prepare him for organ donation.

Like a plane going down, we all tailspin out of control. After the initial shock wears off, my girlfriend becomes suicidal, and our son continues to nosedive into depression.

We bounce back and forth, from my best friend accepting my calls and visits to turning me away, saying it hurts too much to talk to me and she doesn't know if she can ever see me again. Our son drops out of school, starts to self-medicate, disappears for hours at a time or won't get off the couch.

My husband and I insist on counseling for the three of us; our son, a shell, as he sits in the therapist's office. Every now and then I see a spark of light in his angry green eyes, only to be extinguished so quickly that I'm sure I imagined it.

Most days not one of us wants to get out of bed. It's so much easier to pretend that it's a lazy Sunday morning. But my instinct to protect pushes me up and out into the kitchen to make coffee and breakfast, in order to help my son, if not myself.

One day, the walls of our 3,900-square-foot home are crushing me. I ask my husband to take a drive up to Payson, Arizona with me so I can check out a center I've heard about. It's been some time since I led a yoga retreat, and my students have begun to ask. I'm thinking it might be a positive focus.

We're a little early for our appointment with the director, so we take a walk around the property. Spying a gentleman painting one of the fences, we stop and chat. Two hours and several cups of tea later, he writes his phone number on a piece of paper, saying he needs a helper, and to have our son give him a call.

A Viet Nam vet, he mentors our son with his strong, steady hand and kind, loving heart. For over four years he offers him guidance, trains him in the painting profession and creates a sense of stability that neither his dad nor I can provide for him at this crucial time. His outside- the-family friendship serves as a life preserver, holding him up until the day our son slowly begins to see the possibilities of his own future, while still mourning the loss of his best friend.

~

We're sitting outside the RV, sipping coffee at a campsite in Zion National Park. Overhead, a bald eagle soars, wings spanning against the reddish-orange of the mountain spires. My husband looks over at me, "What?" When you've been married close to thirty years the way we have, you only have to look at your partner and read the conversation that's expressing itself across the planes of their face.

"Nothing. It's weird. I feel so at peace. Happy. Humbled."

He just smiles. That's the thing about my husband. He's better than I am at these kinds of things. I would have said, *See, I told you so.* But he doesn't. He just lets it be, and allows you to figure it out for yourself. No need to be right. But don't get me wrong – he has his foibles just like the rest of us. Thank goodness. But on this point, he's good.

We've been RVing for about ten years now. Last year, we upgraded the Monaco we owned to a 2003 Dutch Star that takes the mountain roads a little smoother and faster than thirty miles an hour. Traveling in a motor home is a life unto itself. A subculture. From couples wearing matching outfits to full-timers who have sold all their belongings for the lure of the road, Kerouac style.

We have been adventuring up the coast of California and Oregon to the canyons of Utah and Arizona. God's country, some might say. But it's not without its hazards. Brakes burning out on top of a Colorado mountain peak. Air bags decompressing while driving sixty-five on a two-lane highway in the middle of Bumfuckwia. And of course, the minor catastrophes like the windshield wiper blades breaking apart just as the storm hits its zenith.

After a time, you learn to go with the flow. Adapt and adjust the plan to your surroundings, and what's happening in any given moment.

We were pretty new at it the year we drove from Phoenix up the California and Oregon coast. With our son Steve, and Max the race dog, it took Steve three days to make it to Portland, breaking up the drive with a stop in Sonoma to watch an Indy car race.

I flew up and met them in Portland. We spent a week together at a campsite near the Tualatin River, umbrellaed by oak, pine, maple and Oregon ash trees, the air intoxicating. At the end of the week, our son flew home while Steve stayed in Portland to visit his family and friends. And I drove to The Breitenbush Hot Springs for a four-day yoga retreat.

Not ever a "real" camper, I was totally stretching it staying in a one-room cabin, two single beds, with a woman I'd never met. It did have a toilet and sink. Down the trail about half a mile, we shared an outside shower stall with about thirty other people – three flimsy plywood walls and a curtain for privacy that blew open with the breeze.

It was hot, humid and glorious. Yoga and meditation every day. Vegetarian meals. The river to cool off in during the day and the hot springs at night. We arranged for Steve to pick me up on the morning of checkout.

After saying goodbye to my teacher and friends, Steve turns to me and asks, "Where's the hot springs?"

We take a little walk and I show him. He looks around. Looks at me. "Everyone's coming out with only a towel on."

"Yeah."

"Did you go in naked?" Sounding a little bewildered and intrigued.

"Yeah."

"You want a take a dip before we take off?"

We drop our clothes and in we go.

~

Life on the road is a metaphor. You can pretend you're in control, but we all know how well that works. So, you do the best you can. You prepare. You set yourself up for success. Buckle your seat belt. Say your blessings. Then you let go and engage life.

From the hot springs, we slowly make our way down the coast. Our first stop is Trinidad, in Northern California. We plan to stay for two days to rest and regroup.

Late in the afternoon, on a gray, misty, forty-eight-degree day, we pull into Sounds of the Sea RV Park. We hop out to assess the place before hooking up. No sound. No ocean view, as promised at our prepaid and supposedly premier spot.

It's a small park. Maybe thirty-five sites. And all but about six of them are old fifth-wheelers and RVs, tireless and set up on blocks. None of these vehicles have seen the open road in God knows how long.

"Does that sign near the laundromat say to register your name at the office if you're carrying a firearm?"

That night I toss and turn. Every twenty minutes I ask, Steve, *are you awake?* His response, "I am now." I'm convinced someone is going to barge into the RV aiming a semi-automatic handgun in our faces. Early the next morning, we look at one another, and in silent agreement we pack up and head out.

We're even more exhausted than before we stopped for the night, and now we don't know where we're going. We open up our *Woodall's RV and Campground Directory* searching for another park. Nothing.

Finally, Steve makes a right onto a sleepy dirt road that heads west. "Where in the heck are you going?"

"I have a feeling."

"I'm not sure that's comforting."

It's another dreary day, and at this point, all I want is to find a place that feels safe to stop.

It's slow going, because the narrow dirt road has morphed into sand as we wind and climb upward. Rocks sit in the middle of my belly. Trying not to scream, I wrap my arms around myself and hug tightly as I lean in towards the middle of the RV. As if that will help shift the load.

We take a tight turn, and as we straighten back onto the road, in the near distance, the ocean appears. The road takes another turn, slightly to the left, where we spy a little sign with white letters: State Park. Overnight camping allowed.

We're on a bluff overlooking the ocean. The sweet, earthy fragrance of the eucalyptus trees creates a shady canopy overhead. I help guide Steve into a spot that backs up to a wide-open field that appears to go on for miles.

Quickly we secure Max on his leash, fling open the door and walk down from the bluff to the ocean. Only a handful of people are strolling the beach. The tension oozes out of my body with each step and each breath I take. Pausing, I turn my face up to the moist salt air, allowing the ocean breeze to carry away all thought except my "I am" breath. I am safe. I am at peace.

The next morning, we wake to the sound of murmuring voices and a swishing sound I can't make out. Steve calls to me from outside the RV, "Come and see this."

The field behind us is filled with rows and rows of luscious, ripe strawberries that at that very moment are being hand-picked and tossed into bushels. We wave to the workers and they wave back. Walking to the very edge, we each pick a strawberry, rinse it off with our water from our bottles, pull off the stem and pop it right into our mouths.

~

Truth be told, it took me a while to settle into being on the road in a forty-foot RV, trailing a car behind us. For the first few years it was as though I was traveling in an oversized outhouse on wheels. Saying I didn't like it is an understatement.

I don't know when the RV ownership bug really took hold of Steve. But it was about nine months after our loss when it came to the surface.

~

We're all still walking around, loose bones held up by feverish skin. Trying our best to make sense of how to live without the love and physical presence of our precious young man. Our life clearly defined now – before we lost him, after we lost him.

One Saturday afternoon, I enter the office that Steve and I share, when it hits me that every time I walk nearby, he quickly minimizes the screen and flashes something else up.

What the hell. Is he having an affair? I really don't need this right now.

"Okay, spit it out. What don't you want me to see?"

He's got that look. "Motor homes." And right there before my eyes, popping up onto his forty-three-inch monitor, appear too many RVs to count.

"Okay, next question. Why?"

"I've been thinking it might be fun to buy one."

"Are you kidding me? It's a waste of money. They not only come with a hefty price tag, but they're a fortune to run and maintain. Nope. No friggin' way."

The not-so-clandestine search continues. It shouldn't be so surprising. For the past eight years, he's been renting RVs and driving them out to his beloved car races. Spending the weekend with the guys, hanging out. Camaraderie and all that. My belly drops.

Sure enough, I'm along for the ride and we're walking through a 1995, thirty-eight-foot, one-owner, Monaco Dynasty diesel pusher. Supposedly, in RV jargon, that's a really big deal.

Later that night, we're weighing the pros and cons, and I'm not getting a good feeling. "What is it with you and RVs anyway?"

"I don't know."

"No; after everything we've been through, that's just not good enough."

He closes his eyes. Takes a few deep breaths. Looks over to me and whispers, "Freedom. It represents freedom."

~

Our inaugural longer-than-a-weekend trip is Park City, Utah. The evening we arrive it's raining so hard we can barely see. It's the middle of July and it's cold. Dark. The forecast calls for the next two days to be more of the same. So, like it or not, Steve wraps up in his rain gear and braves it in order to get us hooked up with water, electricity and sewer. I stay warm and dry inside and begin to make a light dinner.

We've made this trek so that I can serve as one of my teacher's assistants at an Immersion Training he's giving. I'm excited and a little nervous. As it turns out, we do little assisting, and more observing – which in fact is an extraordinary experience. At different intervals during the training he instructs the students to form groups of six, and invites the assistants to sit in as guides to the group.

The participants are a mix of new and seasoned teachers who wish to take a deeper dive into the study of yogic teachings, both the methodology and the philosophy. Among other topics this particular immersion will study, from a Tantric perspective, are the seminal Hindu scripture, *The Bhagavad Gita, The Song of the Blessed One.*

~

The Bhagavad Gita is an allegory that takes place on the battlefield of Kurukshetra or Dharma. While Dharma has several meanings and nuances, it's translated here to mean duty or righteousness. This epic tale can be thought of as a "snapshot in time" within a greater story. Here, on the field of Dharma, Prince Arjuna asks his charioteer Krishna, who's also his best friend and brother-in-law, to stop – right smack dab in the center of the two opposing armies. Both sides are made up of friends and family, which adds another element of confusion and pain.

As a result, Prince Arjuna experiences a complete meltdown. He wishes to turn his chariot around, take his bow and his arrows and go home. The pesky problem is that Arjuna and his brothers no longer have a home to return to. The war is the result of the narcissistic greed and nihilism of his jealous cousin Duryodhana, who leads the opposing forces.

So, a conversation ensues between Krishna and Arjuna, where Krishna slowly reveals to Arjuna that he, Krishna, is in fact God.

Over the course of the conversation, Krishna introduces the three great paths of yoga, Karma – action, Jnana – self-knowledge, and Bhakti – devotion. He also presents the concepts of success and failure, the necessity of courage in living one's Dharma – duty and the practicality of everyday life.

The Gita, as it's fondly called, is a story filled with subtlety, paradox and the grave questions we all ask ourselves at one time or another on the battlefield called life. It's a story in response to life's chaos, and the moral ambiguities and questions we face. What is the nature of God? What is my essential nature? How do I navigate in a world that pulses and breaks apart? How do I make skillful choices? What are my responsibilities? What is my place in the world?

The Gita is one of the most revered texts, both in India and the West. For its timeless beauty lies in its directive of our shared humanity.

~

It's the end of the fourth day of the five-day training when my teacher asks the assistants to come up to the front of the room. He introduces us all again and shares a little anecdote about each of us. When it's my turn, he informs the group that my husband and I have been dealing with a family crisis. And he's proud of the way I've been handling the burden. Then he asks me how I'm feeling. I tell him I am doing my best to take the pain and turn it into something creative. But that it's hard. The truth is that I have good days and not-so-good days. I still feel sad. Torn apart. My heart shattered. My trust betrayed. I'm Arjuna.

He looks me in the eye and says, "Paulette, take it to the highest."

We say that a lot in my community. Take it to the highest. I know how to do it intellectually, but how in the hell does it really happen? I offer it into the fire of consciousness during my meditation practice, and ask for the pain, for the situation, to be transformed. And I wait.

Over an early dinner after the last day of training, I share with Steve yesterday's discussion. Since we're both living it, I know he needs to hear this too. After our meal, we walk hand in hand. Somewhat aimlessly, we window shop.

"Look." I point to a sandwich sign advertising tram rides up the ski slope. It's eighty-two degrees and sunny. "Let's do it."

"You're afraid of heights."

"I know, but what better way to take it to the highest?"

The chair begins its ascent, and at first, I can't look out. I stare at my hands – one gripping the bar and one squeezing Steve's. I begin to murmur out loud, "Soften your skin. Now open to Grace. Soften your skin. Now open to Grace. Soften your skin. Open to Grace."

As the chair continues its rise, I lift my gaze and look out over the town and the snow-peaked Wasatch Mountain Range in the distance. We're let off at the top and walk into a meadow of bright, sunny wildflowers, bowing their heads just for us. We hike along the groomed trails, marveling at the beauty and the metaphor. Standing in the meadow looking out for miles, I feel tears sting. Yet my breath smooths out. My skin does indeed soften, and my heart opens.

That day began my love affair with exploring the Sonoran Mountain Preserve near my home. Hiking the

Apache Wash Trail became my go-to for anything that ails my heart. It's the balm that soothes and softens as I walk to the top of the lookout, so that I might take it to the highest and set my burdens free.

~

My mom and I are sitting in the doctor's office. A specialist in breast cancer. In fact, the doctor we're waiting for is a surgical oncologist who has come highly recommended.

I'm trying to put my brave face on. Especially since my mom is doing the same. Taking hold of her hand as if it were a wounded bird, I gaze down. Squared-off nails. Crepe-paper skin, almost bursting through with knotty blue veins. Large knuckles. Peasant hands. I'm struck that it's hard to distinguish my hand from hers. When did that happen, I wonder. I tenderly squeeze, then let up quickly, afraid I'll break the delicate bones and choke the life force right out of her.

A forty-ish-looking woman walks in, wearing comfortable yet stylish black shoes. A plaid wool skirt and black sweater. No makeup. Her naturally pretty face instead wears compassion and kindness. She introduces herself, and pulls up a chair in front of us. Barely an inch between my mother's knees and the doctor's knees. The doctor leans forward and looks directly into my mom's eyes. She is present. Clear. Direct.

As I let go of my mom's hand, the doctor swiftly takes my place. Intently, she asks my then eighty-eight-year-old mother, "Do you have any questions?" My mother does.

"What if I do nothing?"

"Oh, I really don't see that as an option."

Occasionally, one or the other glances my way. Q and A takes about thirty minutes. This doctor appears to have no other patient in the world – though I know that's not true, as we saw many a pained face in the waiting room. For a few more minutes, they simply chat about ordinary life stuff.

Then the doctor turns towards me, "Do you have any questions?" Nodding, I flip open my notebook and begin my litany. Remaining calm and unhurried, as if she has nothing more pressing to do, the surgeon responds.

Next, she guides my mother to the examining table. As she helps her to lie back, the doctor casually looks over her shoulder.

"What do you think your mother's secret is in being such a vital and vibrant eighty-eight-year-old woman?"

I pause. Open my mouth to speak. I'm smacked in the gut. Instead of coherence, blubber erupts.

She hands me a tissue. "I'm sorry. Was that a painful question?"

"No. Yes. I mean… It's a beautiful question."

And for weeks I could not stop contemplating. It set off a maelstrom.

As a first-generation Italian-American, my mother embodies some darn good genes. She grew up with immigrant, uneducated parents who came to the United States to make a better life for themselves. They were hardworking, industrious people who loved and lived with grace and grit.

At thirteen, she rode the bus after school into downtown Chicago to work, and help support the family. She was feisty. Still is. Rebellious. Smart. Joyful. If given the opportunity for higher education, she would have graduated with high honors. And I'm convinced my mother would have been one of the first high-earning female executives. Instead, she raised my three brothers and me while running a small business with my father.

This is what I believe. My now ninety-year-old mother remains vital and vibrant because she continues to cultivate curiosity. For life and for people. Her heart is generous, kind, compassionate. Life was not always easy. Like most of us, she has ridden the roller coaster. At her age, her experience of loss is great. As a result of deep pain, my mother's appreciation for this gift of life is ever present.

One recent September, she joined her next-door neighbor, an old-world gentleman also ninety, to watch in wonder the solar eclipse and the Blood Moon. The neighbors in the close-knit enclave where she and my dad lived for thirty years had fondly designated her "The Mayor." She's the go-to girl for a cup of coffee or an unburdening of your sorrows, and a mediator for all the "he said, she saids." My mom throws together meals for sick friends faster than most people think about doing it.

Just last week, one such neighbor expressed how much she appreciated my mom's forthrightness. She cried to her, and expressed that if she had known my mom as a young girl, she would be a more confident woman today.

When my mother feels she has transgressed, an apology comes easily. Her sense of humor delights. Her vibrancy and vitality are the result of the way she views life.

We call that darshan in the yoga world. Darshan is your world view – the lens in which you see life, yourself and others. Darshan is setting your eyes on the target of your intentions. It's your personal philosophy and your vision of reality. Darshan is the agency that fuels your actions.

My mother's darshan is to receive life on its own terms. Never forgetting that it's a privilege, she enjoys the rich diversity of being human. She is a yogi in the truest, most profound sense of the word.

Her mastectomy was performed two years ago on the day before Thanksgiving. My youngest brother was in town with his family for the holiday. He of the plaid baby carriage. Together we brought her to the hospital, helped settle her in as she waited for the surgery, and then sat side-by-side in the family waiting room, neither one of us wanting to voice our fear. So instead, we squashed it. He texted. I read.

Five hours later, we're told we can go to her room where she's being brought up from recovery. They wheel her in and carefully place her in bed. She's still groggy but knows we're there.

"Is it over?"

"Yes," in unison.

The nurse talks to the three of us, going over a few things, making sure my brother and I understand. She looks over at our mom, "Can I get you anything?"

"I'm dying for a cup of coffee. And can you please make sure it's fresh."

~

Growing up, and into my early adult life, I struggled to find my voice. A lot of women do. For me it's been a dance of concealment and revealment. When I speak, there's a revelation that happens. A window opens, even if ever so slightly. Words expressed become patches of torn flesh. My throat clamps shut, sealing the passageway of vulnerability.

Speaking what's on my heart is like exposing the Wizard behind the curtain. It's actually me, sitting there with Dorothy, Tin Man, Scarecrow, Lion, Toto, the Wicked Witch of the North and the Good Witch Glinda. The reality is that I am all of those characters. Distinct parts of me revealed in the light of day. And so is each of you.

When I share, with my teacher-training students, stories of how shy I was in my younger years, they laugh and think I'm kidding. I'm not. My insecurities held me prisoner inside my own body, mind and heart. Sometimes I felt trapped behind hard, cold barbed wire. The practice of asana was the initial breaking-through. Then the dive into the teachings of yoga began an even greater letting go of the chains in which I bound myself. Often, they were like silken scarves that only needed a slight movement in order for me to ease them away.

In the tradition of yoga, there's a concept called Matrika. Its literal translation means "little mothers," and it refers to the letters, sounds and syllables of the Sanskrit language. In the yoga world, sound is considered to be the source of all life. Matrika Shakti is thought to be the creative power of sound, speech, voice, words. A vibration arises from your voice and an action emanates from it.

Oftentimes I ask myself, do my words align with my action? Like the cliché, "Am I walking my talk?" Matrika can limit you or set you free. It can bring someone closer or push them away. Matrika Shakti is the power of subtle messages that affect one's darshan.

It is no wonder that I was called to this profession. You are often being led to that which presses you to the edge of comfort. Whether to remain stuck, self-imprisoned by your false beliefs, white-and-black thinking, cultural and socio-economic imprinting, the choice to remain or break away and apart is yours.

Over the years, I have bumped up against myself in myriad ways. Pushed back against the growth I sought. At the same time, I melted like ghee in permission. It's not a straight and narrow path to enlightening moments and transformation. It's not fixed. But like the nagas, or serpents, in the Tantric myths, you're invited to take the road that curves and bends, sometimes losing sight of the beginning – and at the same time knowing there's really no end. You simply slide on your belly along the serpentine route that is your life.

As the once-shy one in the crowd, I was a back-row kind of girl. Not looking for attention, while at the same time wearing outrageous tie-dyed clothing, screaming out to the world, *look at me, please, will you just look at me?*

That's the rub. This being human is host of complex notions and paradoxes. It's a gift, if only we could pause long enough and see ourselves through the light of compassion.

There are so many moments in life that shift us. Sculpt us. We may recognize it instantaneously, or not know it for what it was until much later. This is one of those moments.

~

I'm in Denver at an advanced teacher training of 250 colleagues. My good friend and I place our mats down next to one another. And surprise, surprise – she's also a back-row kind of girl. Third day into the training, our instructor asks us to stand up and walk around the room in order to find a few people we don't know. I abhor these kinds of exercises. My skin prickles. My mind dulls. I wander around until someone I don't know waves me over. I'm now seated in the front row, dead center in front of the teacher's spot, though at the moment, he's walking around the room talking to people.

Through his headset, his voice calls out, "What's the highest reason we practice yoga? Take five minutes to journal, then turn to the person next to you and share."

Next thing I know, he leans down and asks me what I wrote. I read him back a haiku. He nods. "Be prepared to stand up and read it to the group."

After a few people rise and share what they've written, he whispers to me, "Stand up and face one side of the room and recite the haiku, then turn and face the other side and read it again. Speak from your belly so everyone in the room can hear you. Even the person in the far corner of the room. You can do it."

I stand up and the room swirls in front of me. My friend's face slowly comes into focus and she smiles. Placing a hand on my belly, I take a few breaths. In the distance, "You can do this."

"Seeds of love we plant. It is the highest teaching. From the muck we bloom."

Later, I learn that in classical Japanese recitation, haiku is recited twice out loud.

Chapter Fifteen
~~*Finding Your Inner Guru*~~

We're meeting our son and his long-time girlfriend for a movie and dinner. I call her Angel Girl. Need I say more? It's his birthday, and as our tradition goes, our son gets to choose the movie and the restaurant. No doubt we'll go to his favorite, Houston's, for the knife-and-fork ribs with two sides of fries. Since I don't eat meat, I've never tasted the ribs that call us back year after year. But I do manage to sneak several fries.

They sit across from us in a rounded booth when my mom-radar zones in. My breath catches. I can't quite name it. My blood feels hot under my skin. Maybe because he's nearing the end of his twenties, there's an electricity in the air. A look. A secret smile. I know there's something up with these two. They've been together now six years. Somewhere along that time, I silently invited his girlfriend to step in fully, as it was the appropriate time for me to step back. But that invisible thread that connects me to this young man may be unseen, yet ever strong.

As I look at my family of three, I feel a tightness in my chest, and unshed tears sting the back of my eyes. He's never been an easy kid. His Papa, my dad, says he entered the world with his tiny little hands clenched into fists. Just ready. I believe that could be true. Ready to defend himself against a foreign world.

He challenged every house rule, never went with the status quo and asked questions about life that forced me to dig deep. He's the gift of love I had been searching for during my early years. And, his independence forced me to grow up and show up. To consciously break the pattern of control that I continually fought against. Break away from the old norms and the co-dependency that served no one.

~

In the yoga tradition, there is the concept of "the guru." Guru is a Sanskrit word. Gu (darkness) ru (light). Simply put a guru is the "remover of darkness."

The guru, with a capital G, possesses the power to remove the darkness of illusion from the devotee's egoic mind. In the classical tradition, and even in some of the non-dual traditions of yoga, the Guru is an actual person who has been initiated into a long line of Gurus from those who have come before. The idea here is that through the Gurus' love, and through their grace only, enlightenment is bestowed upon the yogi.

As a lapsed Catholic, this teaching of the Guru mirrored the God on high doling out righteous justice. So, I've struggled with the concept throughout the years. Another way to look at the Guru is to turn the concept on its head. Instead, consider experiences, relationships, teachers, any significant awarenesses as guru moments. For ultimately, spiritual growth and personal transformation always require the practitioner to do the work that stirs the inner crucible of awakening. Like a sunrise that streaks across the sky with fire-orange, purple and grayish pinks. You stand transfixed, and in that moment the personality syncs with spirit and you receive a clear message of your connection to all things. Or, your baby reaches up to you in recognition and a portal opens.

Guru moments may happen when you experience an awakening to your own shadows. Another guru moment is the willingness to bring the shadow into the light of your awareness. And yet another is to then learn how to integrate your shadow in order to be more fully alive and present. Instead of running from your shadow, you turn, greet it and reach out your hand in compassion.

My son has been one of those teachers to me. Wise. Questioning. Pushing boundaries. Pointing to the spacious sky of a new paradigm. Guru moments and pointers are not always easy, but they are oh, so worth it.

The Year of Ten is far behind us now. His original set of *The Chronicles of Narnia* sits among his ever-expanding library. He's a voracious and diverse reader. Science fiction, physics, astronomy, political science. World religions, yoga scriptures, philosophy and psychology. Fantasy novels to biographies.

I can hardly contain myself. I want to burst out, *Come on, you guys – what's up?*

Finally, Angel Girl reaches out her left hand, where his grandmother's pink sapphire ring shimmers on her trembling finger.

They look at one another. At both of us. "We're getting married."

~

I've been trying to avoid this. Why talk about it, I ask myself? What does it serve? But see, it's that shadow I've been writing about. It wants to hide. But if I'm to stay true to the intention of this book, to my Sankalpa, I have no choice. This heaviness, this shadow begs to be spoken about.

~

Four years ago, I'm teaching a segment in an immersion/teacher training. The students are to consider a teacher they respect. Not necessarily a yoga teacher, but someone who has inspired them. Made an impact. They are to write about the qualities that makes this person a good teacher from their perspective.

After the allotted journaling time, a discussion ensues. And the next thing I know, one of the students calls me her guru. But it's as if she's slapped me in the face. I involuntarily slap back.

"I am not your guru. I'm not anyone's guru."

I sound like a crow. Instantaneously I'm thrown back to a year earlier, when a bomb exploded in my yoga community. I'm reacting. Triggered.

"But you're my teacher."

Hearing the innocence and confusion in her voice, I pause. Take several breaths. Remind myself where I am and what my job is.

"Yes, I'm your teacher. And I'm good at what I do. But I don't want to be your guru. What I hope to do is help you learn how to find your own inner guru. I'm an ordinary person like you. I just happen to have studied a lot and learned a lot, and I love to teach. I've been on this journey longer than you have. That's all."

It's a great teaching opportunity, actually. The students are listening intently. They're leaning in. They want to hear more when Guru Girl asks, "Don't you want to be a guru?"

It's hot in the yoga studio, and suddenly I'm chilled to the bone.

"No, I don't. From my perspective, becoming someone's guru is a responsibility I don't desire. Becoming a guru opens the door to grave misconceptions and potential danger. In the guru tradition, in the classical sense, the guru holds the power to your enlightenment. They have something you want. And only through their grace can you receive it. But that's a slippery slope. If they're the guru, just by the very nature of what it means, you can never attain what they have. It's like a dog chasing its tail. So no, I don't want to be a guru. Want I want, or rather what I hope, is that through the teachings I'm sharing with you, you learn to contain, harness and direct the power for your own life."

Eyes bright. Thoughts swirling. Heads nodding, or even more confused.

"But you're one of my favorite teachers. You know so much."

"So, let's go back to the contemplation. What are those qualities you love and respect? Because therein lies the key to your own power. Those qualities, that wisdom you assign to me, are also available to each and every one of you. In fact, you already have them. What I'm doing is helping you learn how to access them."

~

It's February - 2012. I boot up the computer and my inbox is filled with mail from yoga teacher friends. The gossip has been swirling for the last couple of months. Our yoga organization is going down. Our beloved teacher is acting odd. Well, today it hit the fan – and within days, our community, our community of love, is behaving like a pack of hyenas going in for a kill.

Rumor has it that our teacher was misappropriating funds. Acting sexually unethical with students. Not walking his talk. Somewhere in the rock stardom-ness that is the new world order of yoga, he lost sight of what the method he created stood for. What *he* stood for.

Honestly, I don't know for sure what he did or didn't do. What is fact, fiction, or a little of both. All I can do is share what I saw over the years, and how it made me feel. Some of the experiences were so sweet, inspiring and transformative. Some the polar opposite. Others neutral. What I know for myself is that underneath the veneer that was the yoga community I was active in for over fifteen years, our demons were quietly resting.

Sometimes at conferences and trainings, they woke from slumber. A little sleepy, not quite totally awake. But raising their heads. A teacher you've known for years suddenly walks past you as if they've never seen you before. You're not part of the silently forming inner circle. You have nothing to offer their personal rise to the pinnacle. So why bother with a hello? And a conversation, totally out of the question.

While I was studying, teaching, doing the work, a hierarchy was establishing itself, and in one way or another we were each vying for our place – or at the very least, wanting to be acknowledged. Included. Seen. Appreciated. By each other, and certainly by our teacher.

When something so critical as the implosion of a rapidly expanding organization takes place, how can we not look into the radical mirror of honesty and ask ourselves how we were complicit?

While I can't speak for the hundreds and hundreds of teachers in the community, I do wonder in what ways we, both individually and as a group, might have played a part in putting our teacher up on the Guru pedestal. In what ways did we turn a blind eye to what was happening as the community we loved began to unravel? As our teacher's shadow began to rise up and swell, why did we not take the time to turn inward and face our own?

Here's the crux. If you don't find the courage to look at your own shadows and learn how to integrate them into your life, then they lie in wait, ready to strike out at the least expected and most inopportune times, only to sabotage the desires of the heart.

This, this, is an important yogic teaching. Don't hide. Don't hide from your humanness like it's something to feel shameful about. Be compassionate and committed to doing your inner work, so that you learn to alchemize your personal base metals – and turn them into gold.

Chapter Sixteen
~~*Tough Going*~~

Steve and I are in Portland, Oregon, cleaning out his dad's house and getting it ready to sell after his dad's passing. It's spring. A bit rainy, with a few days of sunshine to ease the monotony. Everywhere you go in Portland, residents plant flowers. Gardens of hydrangeas, lavender, impatiens, roses, gardenias. They are either well tended, or left to grow wild. The beauty and fragrance intoxicate.

Steve and his brother are stationed in the garage, removing boxes from the attic. We guess the boxes have been up there for over twenty years. I'm shredding paper in the kitchen. Dust flies in the air around me. One dumpster is overflowing, and number two isn't far behind.

I'm so tired, my body feels like Silly Putty. We're sad. Nostalgic. We're not only dealing with our own play of emotions, but navigating other family members' stuff and trying not to get pulled into the mosh pit. We're doing a job nobody ever wants.

Day three, I start to cough. Day four, the handyman rips off a piece of old siding on the north side of the house. Dry rot. Steve and I have been sleeping just on the other side of the wall. I imagine the spores sneaking into my lungs.

We pack our belongings and move to a hotel. The next two days we're possessed, emptying the house our loved ones lived in for two decades.

By the time we arrive back home to Phoenix, my fever spikes to 103, with a sinus infection slithering in. I try my best to work through it naturally. Slowly, I start to feel a little better. I return to teaching. The fever spikes again.

The quality of my voice has changed. I don't even recognize it. One of my students affectionately calls me Mick, for Jagger, of course. While it's kind of fun to think I sound sexy, I feel like crap, and am therefore not able to enjoy the image.

Pressure from my family sends me to an ENT (ear, nose and throat) doctor. Five rounds of antibiotics later, the fever mostly lets go, but the infection has taken a stronghold, and my digestive system is now in full counterinsurgency. The naturopath I've started to see is perplexed. I've lost track of the number of blood tests. No mold. No pneumonia, despite the cough. No Valley Fever. No HIV. Yes, I was even tested for that. No Hashimoto's. WTF?

Finally, a diagnosis. Epstein-Barr virus. My immune system is so compromised it's as if I'm running on empty. Plus, I'm freaked out. Isn't EBV highly contagious? What about my precious students? Have I harmed them in any way? I'm sad and scared. I'm a detective possessed, searching for clues.

~

One seemingly ordinary Sunday morning, I wake up and pad quietly to the sink to wash my face before my meditation practice. It's before sunrise, and I don't want to wake my husband, so I close the door and turn on a nightlight.

"Steve," my Mick Jagger voice barks out. "Something's wrong. You've gotta wake up."

From head to toe, my body has exploded on itself. Skin eruptions and angry red welts cover every inch of my body and scalp. All different shapes and sizes. I remember this. And as the memory of another time surfaces, my throat begins to close.

Steve throws on a pair of pants and a sweater. Drives to a nearby CVS and rushes back with a box of antihistamines. He rips one out. I pop it in, grab a water bottle, but the swelling in my throat makes it hard to swallow. I choke it down, where it takes up residence in my throat. Stuck halfway down. I can't throw it up, nor can I push it down any further.

Eight hours later, Steve rushes me to emergency, where they run a bunch of tests. Determine they can't help me and ambulance me to the hospital.

After I wake from the emergency endoscopy, the doctor comes into the recovery room. He's holding a round, stainless metal bowl that fits into the palm of his hand. He gives it to the nurse, and then proceeds to check my vitals. My throat is scratchy, but he does most of the talking, so it's okay.

Then he reaches out, retrieves the bowl and shows me the contents. Sitting in the center is the undissolved, white, M&M-sized antihistamine. I feel like tossing my cookies all over again.

It's outpatient surgery, so after a few more minutes, he releases me. Steve is silent as we drive the seven miles home. It's around 1:00 am. We crawl into bed, and though exhausted, I toss and turn, sleeping in short dreamscapes.

I'm shoving handfuls of white, little pills into my mouth. Choking. Moaning. Crying.

Steve touches my shoulder and eases me back.

The next morning, I'm sipping tea when he says, "Now what?" In two days, I'm scheduled to begin co-facilitating a six-month yoga immersion/teacher training. It's something I've been a part of for ten years, so it's not as if I'm not prepared. I've done this before. It's one of the rewards of the profession to work with students at that level.

I shrug my shoulders. He opens his iPad and doesn't say another word. Later that morning, I walk into the bathroom to take a shower. Instead, I sit on the bed with a hand-held mirror and stare into my face. Forcing myself not to look away, I spend several minutes searching.

Maybe I should take a couple of weeks off. I'll start the training, and when we have the holiday break, I'll plan on a few rest days.

I examine the new wrinkles around the corners of my eyes, but lose count. My skin sallow and gray. Okay, it's looking mummified. I'm wheezing. No stamina to get up and into the shower, I throw myself back onto the bed and continue to stare. What the hell happened to you? My brown eyes dull. Where's the Shakti? The Prana? The life-force? What happened to your vitality? Fuck!

I don't know how long I lay there until I drag myself into the shower. Water rains over the top of my head. Warm. Soothing. Releasing. I invite the tears that I've been holding back for who knows how long to finally flow.

Putting on a clean set of sweats, I walk over to my puja and pick up the framed photo of the goddess Durga from the altar. I light a candle and take my seat, cross-legged in my meditation chair. Breathing is difficult, but I take my time. Inhale a little. Exhale as much as I can. No forcing. Inviting the breath to lead me.

Durga rides a lion, and in her eight hands she wields a conch shell, thunderbolt, sword, lotus, bow and arrow, trident and discus. She's beautiful yet ferocious, and beholds the world through three eyes: past, present and future. She's called the "Goddess of Tough Going," and since I'm in serious need of her superpowers, I invoke her.

Durga is fierce, intelligent and compassionate. The lion she sits atop represents confidence and strength. The symbolism of the sword she holds I especially need now. With her keen intelligence, Durga slices through the BS – revealing truth. She braces herself for battle as the Mother of All.

After taking in the sight of her, I begin to chant one of her many mantras. "Om Dum Durgaye Namaha." Until the chant opens up into silence. I'm not sure how long I sit.

Finding Steve, I say, "I need to step away from teaching. Today. Not next week. Not two months from now. Today."

"I know."

~

Later that day, I make arrangements to take a sabbatical. Well, that's what I tell myself. My family. Friends. Students. I'm taking a sabbatical. As if I've been thinking about taking time off from teaching for a while. As if I have a project planned, and taking a sabbatical provides me the space and time to do so. As if I'm on paid leave.

After I make the decision, and put things in motion to have my teaching obligations taken care of, my Eveready Battery finally loses its charge. The illness takes the lead. Most nights, I toss and turn with heart palpitations that feel like anxiety, but are actually a physiological effect of the EBV. The virus stimulates the nerves in my feet, and they cramp into little balls. Many nights, drenched in sweat, I throw the covers off, change my pajamas and shiver with chills. About four in the morning I finally fall into a chaotic sleep, and can't get out of bed until 8:00 or 9:00 am.

A few weeks later, I run into a colleague of mine in the grocery store. I ask her how she's doing.

"I'm doing well now. But I had to take time off from teaching, because I had the Epstein-Barr virus. Actually, the virus never really goes away. But I found a great naturopath familiar with the illness. It's in dormancy now."

Right there, in the organic produce section, I begin to cry. I've felt so alone. Helpless. But now someone else gets it. "What's her name? Do you know if she's taking new patients?"

A lifeline appears. My friend grabs her cell phone from her bag and quickly scrolls to find the doctor's number. We chat for a few more minutes, and when we hug goodbye, she gives me a little squeeze. "Be kind to yourself. It takes time."

One of the first things my new referred doctor, who specializes in virology, tells me is that the Epstein-Barr virus is one of the most misdiagnosed and misunderstood illnesses.

And, "You're not contagious. You haven't been for years."

She devises a protocol. Advises me that there are no quick fixes, and that I need to learn to be patient with the process.

Ha! Another thing I learn is that EBV and chronic fatigue syndrome are not psychosomatic illnesses. Or for couch potatoes. But generally speaking, those who struggle with these types of maladies are usually the opposite. Motivated. On fire. Purpose-driven to a fault.

The journey is circuitous. Winding around the curves of self-care, healing, relapse, healing, patience, self-honesty. A turn here, a slide there, all the while coming home to myself.

My diet is strict, to eliminate as many chemicals and toxins as possible. Lots of organic vegetables and wild salmon. That's pretty much normal, so no biggie there. But I learn I'm allergic to eggs, cauliflower, string beans, cane sugar and dairy, to name a few.

Most physical activity stimulates the virus, so my asana practice is reduced to child's pose. Hiking is out of the question. And truth be told, I can hardly walk a block without needing to stop. My legs shake and my balance is off. I'm dizzy and weak. Meditation and mantra save my sanity.

My mood swings like a pendulum. I sleep a lot. On a good day, I fantasize about all the things I'm going to accomplish when I get better. I read a lot of recipes and try baking. Vegan. No cane sugar. So many flops that I tailspin into a chocolate binge. Then start all over again.

One day as I'm pulling banana-pecan muffins out of the oven, I almost drop the pan. Thunderstruck, I place the pan on the counter to cool. I sit at the kitchen table. I'm not on sabbatical, for crying out loud. I'm not working on a special project. I'm on an unpaid sick leave. In a flash, I realize that I've been telling myself and everyone else that I'm on sabbatical, because it was just too much for me to admit how sick I really am.

I journal. Meditate. Sit with it. By now I'm able to walk a little farther. Short hikes. So, I get outside and move through it. The conversation in my head goes something like this: *You're ashamed that you're sick. You feel responsible. As if you did something wrong. Willed it on yourself. You must have some pretty shitty karma. You feel shame because you're a yoga and meditation teacher. A damn life coach. You teach mindfulness. You should know better. You should have seen this coming. You should have been able to do something. You shouldn't be ill.*

I turned on an internal faucet and the "shoulds" came pouring out – leaving me empty of self-recrimination, and ready for a deeper, more compassionate self-reflection.

The yoga I ascribe to doesn't promote self-flagellation. It's a yoga for everyday people, living regular lives. Like getting married. Enjoying sex. Raising children. Going off to work and paying bills. It's called the householder tradition. Instead of trying to overcome the body and its humanness, it teaches that life is a juggling act filled with paradoxes, for which you say yes to life. With all its possible outcomes. Accepting that you will enjoy successes and be willing to pick yourself up after each failure. Because both will happen. No doubt about it.

It's a yoga that promotes learning. And failures are nothing more than opportunities for more learning. This yoga teaches you that you will indeed have desires. It is a part of the human condition. So instead of fearing and trying to extinguish your yearnings, it's more valuable to learn how to prioritize them. The yoga teaches you how to turn your shadow into advantage and grace. How? By accepting the shadow, which is really a conglomeration of all your "shoulds." Then integrate them. Turn them into a creative expression of who you are. Turn them into art.

So, yet again, I dive deeply into the teachings, and slowly begin to sip the elixir of my yoga – that I may accept where I had been and acknowledge what might yet be possible. Little by little. Day by day. Again and again.

Chapter Seventeen
~~*Sitting in the Middle of the Paradox*~~

I wonder: Just how many times does a daughter have to sit with her ninety-year-old parents and discuss what their resuscitation wishes are? For the love of God, enough already. As we sit in the doctor's office for the gazillionth time, I realize that their Advance Directives need to be updated.

We're here again at the Veterans Administration at the advice of my dad's primary physician. She's suggesting palliative care, so today's appointment is with yet another new doctor. Once again, we're going through a list of questions and answers that I thought we'd given and were documented. Apparently not.

The calm and kind doctor directs the questions to my slightly cognitively impaired father. Among his many illnesses: kidney disease, sugar diabetes, cancer survivor, recipient of a TAVR heart valve, familial tremors. Most recently, he's been diagnosed with mild vascular dementia, though the hard truth is that we've seen the changes happening over the last few years.

He's struggling to answer the question, "If the cardiologist found that your new valve was leaking more than it is, and they recommend undergoing another surgery, would you want to do that?" She patiently explains the pros and cons, states frankly that the risks for someone his age are great, and with the consideration of his overall health, that his chances of survival are slim.

My dad looks to me. Then to my mother. My mom gives me a nod and I ask the doctor if I can help. I alternate between acting like the parent and regressing to a twelve-year-old. Finally, my ninety-year-old mother intervenes.

"We've been married for sixty-seven years. I've known him since we were seven." She looks over at my dad. "He and I have talked about this. You know, before...."

Even in his younger years, it was as if he needed a kick start to get the words rolling. Now, it's like a car engine that won't turn over the first two or three times. Just about when you're ready to give up, it revs and accelerates. Some days, I wish I could find that magic brain solenoid and help him ignite. Other days, I wish I possessed mental telepathy and could will his thoughts to flow coherently. And then, on "bad daughter" days, I'm impatient. Sharp. Disappointed in myself. Down and dirty sad.

Yesterday he was seventy years old, driving a van for the Scottsdale Plaza Hotel, making runs between the hotel and the airport. With a side gig, entertaining elders at group homes through a nonprofit organization. Two to three times a week, he'd load up the trunk of his Lincoln Town Car with an old, battered card table, a karaoke machine and two cordless microphones to visit group homes and sing his favorite tunes from the Big Band Era.

Today, he's ninety. After this initial appointment with the palliative doctor, I'll wheel him down the long, narrow hall, my mother holding on for support, then maneuver the oversized VA chair onto the elevator, get off on the second floor and head to the physical therapy clinic to pick up his brand-new portable walker.

~

It's 4:19 am Mountain Time and I can't sleep. Memories rush through me like a raging river. Steve and I are visiting our friends in Ivins, Utah. We haven't seen one another in almost a year. After twenty-four years of living in their Scottsdale, Arizona home, they packed up their furniture, the portrait of their beloved, deceased son, their seventeen-year-old Jack Russell Terrier, and made a soul-saving geographical move.

Holding themselves together with their very last strand of slippery hope, they left the home that whispered their son's name in every corner. The sacred space where our kindergarten Tiger Cubs carved pumpkins outside on the patio. The yard where we held a coming-of-age sweat lodge for our boys. Pizza nights, talking circles, sleepovers, birthday parties and World of Warcraft marathons.

~

Their new home sits on a bluff overlooking a gulch and the majestic red rocks of Snow Canyon. We walk the natural stone path to the edge of their two-acre property and stare down the hill. The gradient shades of green shrubs shimmer against the red-clay dirt. When the rains come, the gulch fills and waterfalls appear overnight. It's a birdwatcher's paradise. A vulture soars overhead, then dives for its prey. Rabbits scurry in hiding or stand shocked still. The silence is as vast as the vista.

I look to my left, and out in the distance I catch a glimpse of a swift-moving animal. "Look, over there, do you see it?" They shake their heads no. It disappears so quickly that for a moment, I wonder if I imagined it. And in the next breath I hear the echo of my teacher's voice, "Grace is saying yes to the experience." I close my eyes, and the beauty of that sleek, loping mountain lion seeps into the fissures of my sorely tender heart.

As we say our goodbyes, my girlfriend pulls me tightly into her embrace. "You don't have to worry about me anymore. I'm happy. I'm really happy."

Chapter Eighteen
~~*Churning*~~

I've been putting pen to paper since I was a little girl. While I have notebooks and files filled with my earlier writing, I did not save even one tiny scrap from those even-earlier formative years. Probably a good idea. Nevertheless, I wish I could touch the hand-printed pages, and read what that child considered important enough to laboriously impress with a sharpened #2 pencil.

I see her, that young girl sitting up high on a pillow. Cane-backed chair pulled up to a round, white, marble table, slashed with streaks of gray and black. The table carefully placed in front and center of the tall picture window in our living room. Floor-to-ceiling beige draperies pulled wide, allowing the milky light of the winter afternoon to filter in. Dirty, packed snow mounds pushed up against the curb, making parking impossible. The barren trees stark against the gloom.

From the kitchen, I hear my mother preparing dinner. Her favorite dented pressure cooker bangs against the stovetop. The sizzle and smell of onions swirls throughout the apartment.

Laid out carefully rest my lined notebook, pencil case filled with yellow pencils, erasers and a brand-new silver sharpener. Flipping the notebook open, my unsteady hand grips the pencil tightly. Sure enough, three words down, snap. I break the tip. I remind myself to loosen my hand just the way Ms. Slater tells me to, on a daily basis.

I sharpen the pencil and begin again.

~

After dinner, plates left on the table, filled with half-bites and vegetables hidden under pieces of bread, I'll squeak my heart out. The youngest still in a high chair, oblivious. Middle Brother, who never sat still anyway, squiggling in his seat.

And Number One Brother dramatically exclaiming, "We have to listen? Again? There's something wrong with her. All she ever writes about is dying. It's morbid."

My mother – I have to hand it to her – commands in the calmest of voices for the entire family to remain seated. "Listen to your sister!" The nanosecond I stop, before I even place my precious lined notepaper down, the two boys grab their plates, push back their chairs and rush out of the kitchen.

"Very nice," one or the other parent might say. Then they too will gather up the remaining dirty dishes for cleanup chores, while I tend to the baby and my tattered self.

Number One Brother, he was pretty accurate, really. I was obsessed with dying. Even as a six- or seven-year-old, I wondered what life was all about. I feared that at any moment someone I knew might get run over by a car. So, what was the point of us being born anyway? Was the planet going to explode? What the heck was I here for was a question I asked myself, and anyone else who dared to listen, over and over again.

Raised in the Catholic faith, I prayed regularly to God to please just take away my fears already, and answer at least one of my questions. Are babies really born tainted with original sin? Why did that little girl get sick with cancer? How come some people are so poor they don't have enough food to eat?

Many a time I was convinced that I heard God's voice instructing me to recite ten Hail Marys and one Our Father – then all would be well. Or maybe it was the priest's voice whose confessional I knelt in every Saturday afternoon – regardless of whether or not I needed to atone for an offense.

While I was unable to express or articulate my angst, I longed to understand the purpose of life. And my place in it. I suppose that's why I began to write. To sort through my feelings and create meaning from the messiness of this existence that pelted my young sensibilities. I suppose it's why I write today.

When I was thirteen, the movie *The Greatest Story Ever Told* was released. For Catholics like us, it was a big deal. A color feature film production. The re-enactment of the life of Christ and his crucifixion. My mother and father, the two older boys and I rode the train into downtown Chicago to attend a Sunday matinee. Later that night, we discussed the movie around the dinner table.

A couple of weeks later, instead of reading yet another story I asked to make an announcement.

"I finally figured it out. I know what I'm here for."

A couple of eye rolls. It was probably my mother who urged me to share.

"I want to be a nun."

I don't know if my brothers laughed or spat out their food, but one of them said, "Are you kidding me?"

"No, I want to be a bride of Christ."

I'm pretty sure it was Number One Brother. "Here she goes again. And what about your new boyfriend? The kid you ride home on your bike from school with every day?"

"What about him?"

"You're going to marry Jesus Christ and him too?"

Honestly, huddled under my covers that night, I imagined my boyfriend's smoldering eyes, and that just about did it for me. I stopped going to church. Stopped writing. And began learning how to French kiss, hiding between the trees and the fence in our yard.

A while later, I picked up journaling again. As time went on, a few writing classes at the community college. Wrote a few pieces. Had them published in a couple of magazines. Start stop. Start stop.

~

A few years ago, during one of my writing spurts, I bumped into a yoga-teacher colleague of mine, who also happens to be a damn good writer. Not to mention a really good guy. We started chatting, and he invited me to teach a workshop at a center he was directing. He was also teaching a writing class for mindfulness.

Out of the blue, he says, "You should write a book."

"Yeah, ya know, I've been working on it."

I sign up for his eight-week class, and sometime in the middle of it, he offers to take a look at the manuscript. My heart, pounding with a fury. Hands sweaty. I push send, and email it to him.

It doesn't take long for him to write back.

I'm not quoting him verbatim, but it's something like, "Paulette, the world doesn't need another self-help book. Your students don't need another self-help book. They need to hear your story. Throw this in the trash and start over."

Tears sting my eyes. I'm not sure if I'm going to throw up, quit the class, or call to thank him. I do none of those. Instead, I drive to the base of the Sonoran Mountain Preserve. Park along the dusty road. Grab my water bottle, and hike my way through the maze in my head.

"He's calling you out, you know. He's asking you to get real. You got the chops for that?"

I didn't trash the manuscript. Because I knew deep in my achy bones that somewhere in that draft of psychobabble a few treasures lay buried. The question became whether or not I was brave enough to excavate them. Then hold them. Sit with them. Until they began to come alive. Compelling me to tell the story I'm here to write.

Being brave didn't mean I wasn't afraid. Scared shitless. It meant I needed to tap into the inner fortitude I frequently forget I possess. Then put one foot in front of the other. Peck one key at a time. Write a sentence. Plant a seedling. Water and nurture it until a root of truth takes hold. Growing deep down into the depths of potential. At the same time, hoping for shoots to push up out of the darkness and reach towards the light.

A million down dogs later and a multitude of students asking me, "What brought you to yoga? Are you vegetarian? What do you have for breakfast? Do you practice every day? Why is meditation so important? Were you always flexible? Healthy? Mindful?" As if.

The thing is, we all have "as-ifs." They're the shadows you want to hide in the closet. But the shadow is composed of pieces and parts of who you are. What I've learned over the years from the Tantric discipline of yoga is that in denying the shadow, you deny yourself. And in viewing this part of yourself as negative or bad is to see yourself as such.

In the Tantric tradition that I teach and practice, the shadow side of the self offers the opportunity to experience greatness. From this perspective, greatness is the ability to live life fully, with all its successes and failures. By not fearing the disparate parts of self, but by welcoming them, we create what's called *sammelana*.

Sammelana is the missing, broken, or extra piece. It's the value-added project. As a result of integrating your shadow, you've actually added more to who you are and what you can offer to your life. This "more" transforms, alchemizes and becomes grist for the mill. The seeds for the garden. Colors on the palette. Cream in the coffee. When you learn to invite all aspects of self to show up, you've learned how to make art of your life. And it is through art that we make meaning of our transient existence.

Over time, I decided to sit my butt down and sort it all out. What initially began as answers to my students' questions soon morphed into a deep excavation of self.

So, this is it. This is the story that refused to go away. That has been churning. Agitating. For as long I can remember.

But it's only a sliver of the story, and it answers only a few of the questions I've been asked over time. The other questions are: So how did you literally do it? What are the strategies you implemented in your life that brought you from the confused, broken, at-times-desperate woman to becoming the person you are today? How did you find strength to go on during the difficult times?

Truly, to fully answer those questions may just mean writing another book. But it is my deepest desire to leave you with a sense of hope and inspiration. So, as you delve into Part IV and return to Kali, I have included a few of the non-pharmaceutical prescriptions I've used over the years. May they be a source of connection. May they bring you peace. May they bring you joy.

However, I want to make it perfectly clear that while I'm no longer desperate, I am at times still confused. And broken. In the Tantric tradition, broken is the gift of being human. It's not something we try to fix and not be. For it is through the cracks and seams of our brokenness that grace flows in and flows out.

Being broken is the way to experience more of life. Broken doesn't mean we're on the ground in pieces – although at times, we certainly may be. It means we're fractal. Pieces of broken light that are capable of shining in many more directions. Being a breakaway man or woman means we've been either taken apart consciously or by circumstances, in order to experience as many faces of the goddesses as we're capable of exploring.

And that, my friends, is the ultimate remedy for loving your life.

KALI
Part Four

"Seeds of Love We Plant
It is the Highest Teaching
From the Muck We Bloom"

Meditations, Contemplations, Practices and Journaling

~~Simple Strategies for Beginning a Meditation Practice~~

Set the Foundation Point of Posture and Practice

As in any discipline, setting a solid foundation is paramount for success. Meditation is a disciplined practice, and feeling successful at it will take commitment and perseverance. Think of it as building a muscle. Below are a few tips that will help you build and sustain a practice.

- Choose a specific place/corner in your home and designate it your meditation space.
- Over time, create a little altar symbolizing that this is your sacred space.

   Decorate your altar by placing a poem, or a photo of a loved one. You can use anything that inspires and lifts your spirit, such as a shell from a favorite beach, etc.

- Choose the time of day that best fits your lifestyle (preferably upon rising, near bedtime, or both).
- Build the practice by committing to three to five days a week.
- Be realistic. Start with five, then ten minutes. Ultimately, you will sit for as long as your heart wishes.
- Set a timer, if you feel that is helpful.
- Sit either on a cushion in a cross-legged position, or in a chair with your spine tall, keeping the natural curves in your back and neck.
- If you're in a chair, place your feet firmly on the ground.
- Move the top of your thighs back. Lift your belly so you feel a toning. This will give you a solid, comfortable base.
- Keep your torso upright, and the sides of your body lengthened, with your shoulder blades snuggled on your back.
- Lift the crown of your head towards the sky. Release any tension in your face and neck.
- Keep your chin level to the floor while drawing it back slightly, and keep the crown of your head over the center of your pelvis.
- Soften your tongue.
- Rest your hands comfortably in your lap with the palms up.

Inner Posture and Basic Dharana or Focus

- Bring your awareness to your inner body. Take a few moments to notice how you feel.
- Scan your outer body. Be aware of the different parts of your body, from the crown of your head to the soles of your feet. Take your time. Feel free to pause and linger along the way.
- Next, bring your attention to your heart center, and imagine this area as a flower, with each petal

unfolding softly. Smoothly. Linger here and enjoy the unfolding of the heart.

- Bring your awareness to your breath. Does it have a quality? A texture? Color? Fragrance?
- Notice the rise and fall of your chest, your rib cage, how the breath enters into the base of your nostrils.
- Rest in the spaciousness of your heart and your breath.

Techniques

From this place of inner posture, breath awareness and mind focus, you can invite in any technique.

- Repeating a word, phrase, sound or mantra gives the mind a job to do. Examples: *Amen. Peace. I Am That. I am strong and stable. I am open and spacious. Om Namah Shivaya.*
- Placing of the hands in a specific mudra or gesture helps to focus the mind's attention. Example: Touch your thumb to the tip of your index finger.
- When a thought arises, simply allow it to do so without judgment. Pause, notice it and let it float on by like clouds in the spacious sky of your mind.
- Allow the mind to say "Thinking." Then let it go.
- Be the witness – simply sit and invite the thoughts to surface.

Again, without judgment: Observe yourself sitting in the chair, in meditation. Then ask:

"Who is watching the meditator? Who is doing the observing?"

Remember that you, the meditator, are developing a relationship with your inner self. As in any new relationship, it takes time to get comfortable. Don't force anything. Let go of expectations, and allow yourself the freedom to be curious. Playful. Creative. Explore and experiment. Meditation should not be another stressor. It is a gift you give yourself.

~~Mantras and Mudras~~

The mantras (sacred sounds) and mudras (hand gestures) that I'm sharing here have been passed down to me over the years from many of my teachers. As there are numerous mantras and mudras arising out of a variety of styles, systems and lineages, they may differ from what you have practiced.

~Malas~

Much like rosary beads used in the Catholic faith, mala beads are considered prayer beads. Today they are also used as jewelry, worn around the wrist or as a necklace.

A classical mala will consist of 108 beads. 108 serves as a sacred symbol for the number of sutras in Patanjali's compilation of aphorisms.

You may chant a seed sound or recite a mantra as you move around the beads. The largest bead, called the guru bead, is not to be crossed over, but with a turn of the hand, you circle around the beads again.

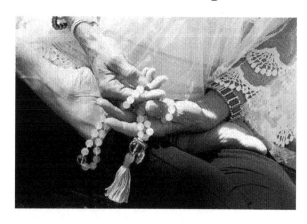

Sankalpa Mudra
~~*Hand Gesture to Seal the Intention of the Heart*~~

Take your meditation seat and invite in three full, spacious breaths. Now with your left hand serving as the fearless and great potentiality that is the goddess Kali, cross her over your courageous heart with unwavering conviction. Rest your left palm, open and receptive, on top of your right thigh. Mindfully fold your right hand, which represents the abundant and ever-fruitful Lakshmi, into the left, firmly pressing the hands together. As you form a bond between them, they crystallize your Sankalpa. Thus entwined, Kali and Lakshmi together become the creative power of Saraswati. In her divine timing, Saraswati weaves your intention through the tapestry of the triad, giving wings to your Sankalpa and setting it free into the world. As you sit in the mudra that is the goddesses, speak your intention out loud three times, and then repeat it mentally until the mantra of your Sankalpa falls away.

Kali, Saraswati and Lakshmi
~~*Mantras*~~

There is no right or wrong way to recite a mantra. However, always take your seat of meditation, and spend the initial moments focusing on your breath. When you feel comfortable, begin to recite the mantra out loud. There is power in audible recitation of the sounds. It's called Matrika Shakti, or the goddess of speech and sound. Because speech and sound are fueled by the Goddess herself, audible expression of the sound and chant sends its essence out into the universe. Then, at some organic point in the mantra practice, the mantra turns inward and you will gently repeat it mentally. After a time, the mantra may simply cease altogether, allowing you to rest in the space of the goddess.

If you use mala or prayer beads, you choose to repeat the mantra as you move through the 108 beads of the mala. Or, if you prefer not to use a mala, you may recite the mantra while holding the mudra.

Kali: *Om Krim Kalikayai Namaha* – I honor and bow to the goddess who destroys and transforms illusion.

Saraswati: *Om Aim Hrim Saraswatyai Namaha* – I honor and bow to the wisdom and creativity that is the goddess.

Lakshmi: *Om Shrim Lakshmyai Namaha* – I honor and bow to the goddess of beauty and good fortune.

~~Kali, Saraswati and Lakshmi Mudras~~

Kali: Interlace the fingers and point the index fingers upwards with the hands level with the heart center.

Saraswati: Touch the pads of your index fingers to the tips of your thumbs, forming a circle. Allow the remaining fingers to open naturally. Rest your hands in your lap, palm down, symbolizing jnana or knowledge.

Lakshmi: Place your hands in Anjali or prayer position. Open your fingers like the blossoming of the lotus flower, while gently pressing the pads of your little fingers together with the inside edges of your thumbs. Rest the flower of your hands near your heart.

Asana: The photos on the following pages are basic postures that will guide you through a beginning asana sequence. Always begin your practice with a quiet centering. Be aware of your breath and set your intention. Upon completing the postures, sit for about five minutes, holding your Sankalpa in the energy of the heart. Then conclude your session by taking Savasana or resting pose.

Note: Before beginning any type of exercise, please consult your physician.

Tadasana
Mountain Pose

"Pull power up from the earth into the pulsating core of the pelvis and stand tall into the Light."

Utansasana
Forward Fold

"Hug the legs together with steadfastness as you fold deeply into yourself and gaze into the depths of your Heart."

Prasarita Padottanasana
Wide Leg Stance

"With conviction maintain steadiness in the legs and courageously look deeply into the unchartered caverns of your Being."

Utthita Parsvakonasana
Side Angle Pose

"From the periphery gather your energy into the power of the pelvis to allow your inner light to shine ever brighter."

Virabhadrasana II
Warrior II Pose

"Confidently embrace the thigh muscles toward the bones and draw up from the foundation. Stand neither in the past, nor the future, but in the present moment."

Utthita Trikonasana
Triangle Pose

"As a star pulses with gleaming light gather stardust from the periphery into the core of your own radiance."

Virabhadrasana I
Warrior I

"Cultivating willpower pull strength up from the foundation into the core center and extend the arms overhead in readiness for your spiritual journey."

Ardha Chandrasana
Half Moon Pose

"Magnetically press into the earth and sip energy up into the container of the pelvis. Offer yourself as a conduit between heaven and earth."

Ardha Chandra Chapasana
Half Moon Sugarcane Pose

"Like the sugarcane, curl open into the back of your heart and taste the sweetness of life."

Parsvottanasana
Intense Side Stretching
Pose

"Root the legs firmly back to gain power from a solid foundation and your commitment to serve will flow forth."

Vrksasana

Tree Pose

"Root the four corners of the standing foot deeply into the earth and ask, 'To what do I root myself into?' In repose await the response of the heart."

Garudasana

Eagle Pose

"Squeeze the legs together in order to invoke the medicine power of the eagle and ask to see from a higher perspective."

Utkatasana
Chair pose

"The power emanating from the pelvis ignites your will to stand in the truth and serve the highest."

Adho Mukha Svanasana
Downward Facing Dog Pose

"Mindfully draw compassion up from the earth into the center of your expanding, vibrating, heart."

Bakasana
Crane or Crow Pose

"Pull into the center of the heart. With the breath expand into the universal and take flight."

Eka Pada Rajakapotasana
King Pigeon Prep Thigh
Stretch

"Powerfully press down to rise up and honor the light of oneself."

Bhujangasana
Cobra Pose

"Like a serpent shedding its skin surrender the bonds clutching at your heart and open to a new day."

Anjaneyasana
Monkey Lunge Pose

"The practice of yoga is to align with the pulsation of life and offer your heart with spaciousness."

Dhanurasana
Bow Pose

"Push, pull, ground down, lift up. Ride the rhythm of Spanda."

Ustrasana
Camel Pose

"Rooting down from the core of the pelvis now feel your chest rise and pulse with gratitude."

Setu Bhandha Sarvangasana
Bridge Pose

"Build a bridge between the breath and the body to receive communication from the source."

Ardha Matsyendrasana I
Half Lord of the Fishes Pose

"Established in your foundation rise up, pause and be present to your life."

Pachimottanasana
Back Extension Pose

"With the breath root down as you extend the spine. With deference soften and let go."

Savasana
Corpse Pose

"Soften your skin, open to the universe and rest in the arms of the Shakti."

The BreakAways

There are moments in life that create a shift, when you consciously or unconsciously break away from an old, tired paradigm that has prevented you from blossoming into the fullness of your potential.

The breakaway moments may be subtle. Often they take shape incrementally. It's a slow dance that results with the dawning of realization that you now are seeing, being, living from a fresh, new perspective.

Breakaways come just as easily when you experience something significant. From crisis to joy. The loss of a loved one. A new job. A move across the country. Marriage or divorce. The birth of a child. It is at these junctures that the armor you have so carefully constructed begins to crack. A little or a lot.

It is precisely in that opening, whether a sliver or a crevasse, that change can occur. When you are faced with the realization that what has previously existed for you is no longer a reality, you are faced with a choice – to either break away and break free, or remain rooted in the muck of your story.

Breakaways are sometimes periods of your life that are accompanied by fear of the unknown. Sometimes it feels more comforting to stay in the reality you know, no matter how stifling or detrimental, than to begin the story anew.

However, take comfort that in the breakaway moments you can draw from the energy of the goddesses that exist within. By embracing their fearless strength, wisdom and beauty, you may begin to explore your inner landscape in order to actualize what's written on your heart. What's important to note is that the goddesses work together simultaneously. They support one another in turn to support you.

This being human is not always an easy ride. This breaking away and breaking into your shadows is a lifelong process that helps you cultivate a more intimate relationship with the self and with others. It is the way of a Tantric yogi – to break away, in order to break in, that you may create a life worth living.

The good news is that breakaways happen over the course of a lifetime. You don't break away once, and then forever be done with growth, evolution, alchemy. While you may want me to say differently, that yes indeed, you experience a breakaway and on you go, it's simply not true. If you choose to "take this mission," this mission of expansion, breakaways become a perfectly natural and amazing way of life.

Another way in which we begin to create the life we desire is through the process of Svadhyaya or self-study. Self-study is a spiritual practice that asks seekers to take a good look at themselves. The ability to self-reflect is one of the greatest gifts of being human. Without it, we are operating only from instinct. Though this has served us well over the centuries, and continues to do so, instinct will only allow us to evolve so far.

The fact is that this planet needs more awakened beings. Beings who, in spite of feeling frightened to get real and honest with themselves, forge ahead anyway. If you're up for the challenge, then I invite you to stay with me here and continue on.

Note: The exercises, meditations and practices in this section may be done all together, or experienced one at a time, giving yourself a day or more in between before moving on to the next one. Some people will want to dive right into the entirety while others will choose to move more slowly, allowing the work to percolate within them. There is no right or wrong way. Follow the nature of your heart. However, please be aware that these exercises are deceptively powerful and provocative. Take all the time you need. There is no advantage in rushing the process.

~~BreakAway Moments~~

Take a comfortable seat and settle into yourself. Sit tall and begin to notice your breath. With focused awareness, breathe in and breathe out several times, until you feel your breath slowing down. Your thoughts slowing down. Your heartbeat slowing down.

Then in the dark void of your mind's eye, drop into a specific time and place when you've experienced a breakaway moment. Don't judge it or try to change anything. Simply allow the memory to surface – so much so that you, as the witness, can feel into the moment.

How old are you? Are you alone or is someone with you? Is it a pleasant memory? If not, don't be afraid. You are only observing, from afar, a moment in time. You're creating a container of safety.

Notice your surroundings. What's your location? What's the weather like? Are you indoors or outside? Is it a summer day? Winter? What are the smells like? How does your skin feel?

Acknowledge why this particular memory is a breakaway. Whatever emotions arise, allow them to be and breathe through them. Breathe in, "I am safe." Breathe out, "I am solid in the here and now."

Sit with the memory until you feel neutral. Sit until you are able to engage all your senses, and yet you've arrived at a place inside yourself that feels no "charge." Nothing inside of you feels triggered. The essence of you is sitting in the theater of your mind, watching a scene from the movie of your life.

Perhaps this one memory has led to another and to another, just like the diamonds of Indra's web in the sky of your awareness. Trust that as a result you have the opportunity to shine ever brighter. Breathe in. Breathe out.

When you feel ready, open your eyes and begin to journal what came up for you. Be sure to capture how this breakaway has helped lead you to who you are today. Be kind to yourself. Be truthful. Be in gratitude. Know that you can return to this exercise at any time.

~~Inviting the Mind to Serve the Heart~~

Continuing on the journey of acknowledging breakaway moments and experiences, you'll now dive deeper into self-discovery and transformation.

Before beginning this next exercise, take at least five minutes to sit quietly in meditation, using the techniques I have shared. This will create a container in which your personal alchemy can take place.

In the Middle Ages, alchemists were known to be chemists and philosophers who sought to turn lead and other base metals into gold. Mystery and imagination have shrouded the concept of alchemy for many years, for their goal was not only to create gold – but to develop the elixir of life.

As a meditation practitioner, you become the chemist and philosopher, turning the base metal or personal demons like fear, anxiety, insecurities, and anger into golden nuggets or assets. Through the purification seat of meditation, you learn how to access and read your private, encrypted files, then turn them into strengths and advantages in order to evolve up the spiral of consciousness.

As I mentioned earlier, breakaways also occur when you consciously begin the study of the self. If you are to break away from the story that is holding you back, then it's important to begin to look through the lens of what is possible for you.

What is possible is that which can be realized. What is possible is that which can happen.

What you do ninety percent of the time truly does matter. What you think will direct the choices you make about the food you eat, how you spend your free time and with whom you associate. These choices affect the course of your life, and indeed alter the probability factor of whether or not you gain access into the world of possibility.

It's a fact that we live at the level of thought and emotion, and that we transform at the level of belief. In the yogic tradition, there's the concept of manas. Manas is a Sanskrit word that means mind. Interestingly enough, manas also means heart. In this next exercise, you will set your intention to sync your mind with your heart in order to acknowledge the ways in which your thinking may be blocking you from living the life you desire.

That's why it's imperative that you take the next step to discover and move through the blockages that continue to trip you up.

I will repeat this instruction throughout the remainder of the book to support you in creating a safe and sacred space.

Sit tall and take three cleansing breaths. Invite the breath to move in and through your body. Release any tension you might be holding in your jaw and neck. Open and close your mouth, and allow your tongue to rest gently against the upper palate. Take a few moments to sit quietly. Whatever thoughts arise, let them surface without attachment. After three or four minutes, mentally ask your inner guidance to take the journey with you as you delve into the next inquiry.

When you're ready, open your eyes, and begin to contemplate and journal the following questions.

- What limiting beliefs are blocking me from realizing the intentions of my heart?
- What past failures frighten me from taking positive forward action?
- What false beliefs are standing in my way?
- What enculturated, familial and social imprinting causes me to repeat self-sabotaging patterns that no longer serve who I am today, my work in the world, and my Sankalpa?

~~Possibilities and Probabilities~~

There is a great Tantric story about the god Shiva and his consort Parvati, and their mutual affinity for gambling. Back in the day the gods and goddesses were known to engage in a competitive dice game that's similar to Parcheesi.

Shiva, being the charismatic, confident dude that he was, always won. Except for the day he didn't. He constantly weighed the possibilities and probabilities of his success, and never entered a game he considered might bring him a loss.

Shiva and Parvati often played the game as if it was foreplay. But since this is a tantric tale, it also inserts a paradox. For Tantra will shake, rattle and roll you. Just when you believe that you have everything all figured out, the myths spin you around and press you to reconsider all you think you know. It is the boon of the philosophy.

So meanwhile, as the story unfolds, Shiva and Parvati are madly in love with one another and enjoy the thrill of the game as if it's an aphrodisiac. However, when it comes down to the dice, they are also fiercely competitive.

One particular afternoon, Shiva, feeling exceptionally cocky, was tempted by his alluring beloved as she batted her eyelashes, giving him a come-hither look.

And in that moment, Shiva's attention wavers – and Parvati wins. She beat the Lord Shiva at his own game.

The idea here of course is to pay attention. Keep your eye on what's possible. Do your best and go for it. Know that if the gods and goddesses can lose a game of Parcheesi, then so can you. Trust that this shouldn't be a deterrent to living a fully engaged life – but rather, that this wisdom may set you free.

At best, life is a game of dice, with glorious wins and a series of failures that ultimately lead you to success. When you learn to uncover these deeply buried barriers and bring them into the light of your awareness, you are better fortified in taking yet another step along the journey of becoming more fully you. You are stacking the odds in your favor, just as Shiva and Parvati did. And, they remind you to keep your eye on the light of your intentions. Stay focused. Be brave, and take the risk of what I call full-throttle engagement yoga.

Crossing over the threshold into the doorway of what is possible for you is the next step in the process. In this contemplation, you will look at and into the seven different aspects that make up your life.

Reminder: Sit tall, and take three deep cleansing breaths. Invite the breath to move into and through your body. Release any tension you might be holding in your jaw and neck. Open and close your mouth, and allow your tongue to rest gently against the upper palate. Take a few moments to sit quietly. Whatever thoughts arise, let them surface without attachment. After three or four minutes, mentally ask your higher self to take the journey with you as you delve into the next inquiry. Open up to the greater vision you hold for yourself; invite your inner guidance to inform you; then journal what insights have arisen.

In each of the categories below, ask yourself, what am I the possibility of, and journal your insights. Use this exercise as a guide to move you forward in your Sankalpa.

~~What Am I The Possibility Of?~~
Are your needs being met in each of the following areas of your life?

Physical/Somatic: The body's ability to sense needs.

Emotional/Discernment: Literacy, to sense and name emotions.

Cognitive/The Mind: Intellect, learning, decision-making and thinking.

Relational/Self and Others: Interpersonal connections and development of intimacy in all your relationships, including the one you have with yourself. Cultivating boundaries.

Spiritual/Connecting to the Web of Life:
1. Belief in a Higher Power.
2. Behaving in a way that benefits a higher group. Agape Love.
3. Appreciative of inter-connectedness of all of Life.

Professional/Vocational: Choices and ethical practices of how to earn your livelihood. Your life's calling.

Integration: The art of becoming multi-dimensional.

~~Guided Visualization for Presence, Gratitude and Grace~~

Take a comfortable seat, either in a chair with your feet firmly planted on the ground, or on a cushion in a cross-legged position. Sit tall and lift the sides of your ribcage, creating a regal posture. Move the shoulder blades on your back without collapsing the torso. Imagine you are taking a sip of cool, clear water. Take the sides of your ears back, and draw your chin in so that it is parallel to the floor. With your spine erect, maintain the natural curves in your back and neck. Feel the stability of your sit bones as you reach the crown of your head towards the sky.

Soften your skin, as if your bones are draped in a silken sari. Relax the muscles of your face. Open and close your mouth to release your jaw. Allow your lips to part slightly, and rest the top of your tongue against the back of your upper teeth. Gently close your eyes and rest your eyelids. Place your hands comfortably in your lap, palms up.

From the top of your head to the soles of your feet, notice how you feel. Discover where you might be holding any tension, and breathe into the area, inviting it to let go.

Now take a deep inhale, and then exhale audibly. Return to softly parted lips as you inhale for six counts, and exhale for eight counts, smoothly through the nostrils. Paying attention to the inhale and exhale, continue this pattern for five rounds. Then allow the breath to return to its own rhythm.

Begin to notice the sounds inside the room. Outside the room. Inside the temple of your body. Take your time. Notice the clothes against your skin. The feel of the chair or the cushion against your legs and bottom. The feel of your hands resting in your lap. There's no hurry. Simply notice. Be aware of the smells in the air. Is your window open to the fragrance of flowers? Are you burning incense or a candle? Now notice the taste in your mouth. Is it dry? Do you taste your toothpaste? Tea? Breakfast? Is it bitter? Sweet? Tart? And now notice what's behind your eyes. The void of darkness. Do you notice any sparkles of light?

Now see in your mind's eye your heart space. Right in the center of your chest. And breathe. Breathe into the front of your heart. Into the back of your heart and into the sides.

As you focus on breathing into your heart center, mentally name one thing, one person, one experience that you are grateful for. Take your time and speak it, first aloud, then mentally. See yourself in that space of time. Remember.

Conjure the memory of gratitude; notice what it feels like. Pay attention and really notice all the parts of you as you continue to breathe into your heart space.

Now, consider where you hope to be in the near future. Working in a career you're passionate about. Living in an environment that uplifts you. Being in a relationship that is meaningful and supports your growth. Feeling comfortable with your finances. Enjoying good health.

Whatever it might be for you, envision it and be in gratitude. Notice again how your body and heart feel.

Maintaining your attention on your heart center, breathe gratitude in. Breathe gratitude out. Breathe gratitude into every cell of your body. Take your time. Stay with the feeling as you continue to breathe. Allow your entire body to rest in this state. Breathing in. Breathing out.

Slowly, begin to consciously deepen your breath, as you draw your awareness into the moment. Into the room where you are sitting. Into the now.

Gently, open your eyes, confident in the awareness that when you are in the state of gratitude, you are in the state of grace. When you're in the state of grace, that which you are grateful for multiplies.

May you be well. May you be happy. May you be at peace.

Glossary

Agape: goodwill, benevolence for self and others

Alchemy: a practice of turning base metal into gold

Anjali: prayer

Anusara: flowing with grace

Asana: posture, seat

ASHY: acronym for Anusara School of Hatha Yoga

Bella: beautiful

Brahma: creator of the universe

Boon: a gift from the gods

Darshan: sight, vision, world view

Durga: the goddess of tough going

Guru: teacher

Hatha: sun and moon, physical postures that balance the body, mind, spirit

Kali: the goddess of manifestation and dissolution

Lakshmi: the goddess of abundance and good fortune

Manas: mind, heart

Mala: garland, prayer beads

Matrika: "little mothers," sounds of the Sanskrit alphabet

Mudra: gesture, seal, stamp

Om Namah Shivaya: to honor the auspicious one, the eternal one that resides within

Parvati: Shiva's beloved

Patanjali: compiler of ancient yoga wisdom called *Patanjali Yoga Sutras*

Prana: life-breath, life-force

Pranam: to bow with respect or reverence

Puga: devotion, worship, altar

Sammelena: broken, missing or added piece

Sankalpa: intention, volition, resolution, will

Sanskrit: classical ancient language of India

Saraswati: the goddess of sequence, time, wisdom, creativity and the arts, a river in India

Savasana: corpse or resting pose

Shiva: auspicious one

Shakti: the primal, creative-force energy

Sutra: short, pithy aphorisms

Svatantra: independent, absolute freedom

Tantra: vehicle or technology for expansion

The Bhagavad Gita: yoga scripture, "The Song of the Blessed One"

Vishnu: sustainer of the universe

Yoga: union

Acknowledgements

After several starts and stops, and what began as journal entries, this book was written over the course of five interrupted years. And without the help of many supportive beings who encouraged me along the way, I'd still be sitting in my writing chair – journal and pen in hand.

My heart is filled with gratitude to my husband Steve for not only urging me to get the words out, but for helping to create the container of time and space, and the setting of nature, in which I could write.

My heartfelt awe goes out to my extraordinary mother and father, who are a testament to what it means to practice yoga off the mat.

Thank you to my brothers, and to the Nordica Kids, whose love I cherish – and our shared memories of joy and sorrow.

I'm in deep appreciation to my teachers, who over the years have offered their knowledge and wisdom with graciousness. A special thanks to Douglas Brooks and Steve Price.

My heart overflows with love and gratitude to my son Steve, who has been one of my most significant teachers.

I bow to my students and clients with humility for the twenty-plus years of entrusting me with their hearts, minds and bodies. Because of each of you, I've strived beyond what I thought was possible.

A special pranam, or bow, to Laurie Hosken, editor extraordinaire, for your keen eye, diligent focus and loving guidance throughout this project.

A ginormous thank you to Nancy Dales for your friendship, creative inspiration and collaboration – not to mention the use of the artful asana and mudra photos.

With deep gratitude to Kimberly Auxier Garofolo for the cover and mala photos and for seeing the beauty in all beings.

Thanks to my *"Determined"* writing friends, and to Tom, Sabrina, Denise, John and the Sojourn staff – without you, this book would never be published.

In the yoga world, the expression Swaha is often used at the completion of a mantra recitation or devotional ceremony. It's one of those words packed with several translations and definitions. In the western world, Swaha is most commonly expressed to mean "So be it!"

In deep gratitude to the Shakti, the energy of creativity herself – Swaha!